William Hamilton Gibson

Eye Spy

afield with nature among flowers and animate things

William Hamilton Gibson

Eye Spy
afield with nature among flowers and animate things

ISBN/EAN: 9783337023737

Printed in Europe, USA, Canada, Australia, Japan

Cover: Foto ©ninafisch / pixelio.de

More available books at **www.hansebooks.com**

EYE SPY

AFIELD WITH NATURE

AMONG FLOWERS AND ANIMATE THINGS

BY

WILLIAM HAMILTON GIBSON

ILLUSTRATED BY THE AUTHOR

NEW YORK
HARPER & BROTHERS PUBLISHERS
1897

Copyright, 1897, by HARPER & BROTHERS.

All rights reserved.

CONTENTS

	Page
A Naturalist's Boyhood	xi
The Story of the Floundering Beetle	1
Fox-fire	11
A Homely Weed with Interesting Flowers	24
Two Fairy Sponges	34
Green Pansies	44
Mr. and Mrs. Tumble-bug	53
Those Horse-hair Snakes	64
"Professor Wiggler"	72
"Cow-spit, Snake-spit, and Frog-spit"	83
The Paper Wasp and His Doings	91
The Spider's Span	104
Ballooning Spiders	112
The Lace-wing Fly	122
The Perfumed Beetles	130

CONTENTS

	Page
Mushroom Spore-prints	136
Some Curious Cocoons	145
Nettle-leaf Tent-builders	154
The Evening Primrose	163
The Dandelion Burglar	171
The Troubles of the House-fly	178
Tendrils	185
A Strange Story of a Grasshopper	195
Riddles in Flowers	202
Luck in Clovers	213
Barberry Manners	221
A Woolly Flock	230
"What Ails Him?"	238
The Cicada's Last Song	246
Index	257

LIST OF DESIGNS

	Page
William Hamilton Gibson	Frontispiece
Initial	xi
Initial. Buttercup Leaves	1
Three Views of a Helpless Beetle	2
Down Among the Buttercup Leaves	3
An Adventurous Baby	6
The Adopted Home	9
Initial. Fox-fire and Fungus	11
A Luminous Fragment	13
Three Specimens by Day.	15
Three Specimens by Night	15
A Fox-fire Bugaboo	17
The Bugaboo by Daylight	21
Initial. The Figwort	24
A Flower with Three Welcomes	29
Sipping the Nectar. Fig. 1	31
In Flight with Pollen. Fig. 2	31
Transferring the Pollen to Stigma. Fig. 3	32
Fifth Day—Pod Enlarging	32
Singular Method of Branching and Flowering . . .	33
Initial	34

LIST OF DESIGNS

	Page
The Rose Mischief-maker	35
The Fairy Using Her Magic Wand	36
The Elfin Sponge of the Oak	39
The Real Fairy of the Oak Sponge	40
The Elfin Sponge of the Brier Rose	42
The Inhabited Rose Sponge	43
Initial. Pansies	44
The Materials	47
Making a Whole Plant Green	51
A Tumbler Concealed Near By	52
Initial. The Sacred Scarabæus	53
Mr. and Mrs. Tumble-bug Rolling the Ball	57
Sinking the Ball	61
Young Tumble-bug Digging out from His Dungeon	63
Initial	64
Amos	66
Dangerous Ground for Grasshoppers and Crickets	69
Busy Grasshoppers	71
Initial. Lilacs	72
"Professor Wiggler" at Home	74
The Lilac Twig in June	75
Tunnelling the Twig	80
"Professor Wiggler" Moth	81
Initial. Grasses and Weeds	83
The Home of the "Spume-bearer"	87
The Real Culprits	90
Initial. A Nest of the Paper Wasp	91
A Wolf in the Fold	95
He was Hanging Head Downward	99
Off for the Paper Nest	101
Initial. Brooklyn Bridge	104
Bridging the Brook	107
From Tree to Tree	109
Initial. Preparing for Flight	112

LIST OF DESIGNS

	Page
Draped in the Glittering Meshes	116
Spider-egg Cocoon	120
Initial. The Lace-wing Fly	122
The Wolf in the Fold	125
A Tempting Aphis Brood	127
Where the Aphides Swarm	128
Initial. A Woodland Path	130
The Perfumed Beetles	133
Initial. A Spore-print	136
Spore Surface of a Polyporus	139
Spore Surface of a Polygaric	139
Method of Making Spore-prints	141
Spore-print of a Boletus	143
Initial. A Nocturnal Bird	145
From a Correspondent	147
The Contents of the Cocoon	149
Where the Cocoon Came From	150
"The Owl on Muffled Wing"	152
Initial. Nettles	154
Leaf-tents of the "Comma" Caterpillar	157
A Design for a Jeweller	160
Initial. The Evening Primrose	163
Two Kinds of Buds	166
The Evening Primrose	167
"The Worm i' the Bud"	168
The Chrysalis and its Moth	169
The Substitute for the Bud	170
Initial. Dandelions	171
The Nest-builder	175
Initial. A Fly Model	178
An Interrupted Toilet	179
An Episode of Fly-time	182
A Victim of Fly Fungus	184
Initial. Sweet-peas	185

LIST OF DESIGNS

	Page
An Impossible and Real Tendril	186
Grape Tendrils Evolved from Blossoms	188
The Star Cucumber and its Compound Tendrils	190
The Prank of a Tendril	193
Initial. An Impaled "Quaker"	195
The Haunt of the Grasshopper	197
The Birth of the Parasites	200
The Two-formed Flowers	202
Puzzling Forms and Faces	203
A. Fertilization of a Flower, as Believed by Grew and Linnæus	206
B. Linnæus's Idea was Wrong	206
C. and D. What Sprengel did not Explain	207
The Way in which the Flower is Fertilized	210
Initial. Clover Leaves	213
A Rowen Field	217
A Five-Leaved Specimen	219
Sleeping Clover	220
Initial. A Barberry Branch	221
"In Arching Bowers"	225
Barberry Blossoms, Showing Sepals and Petals Open. Fig. 1	226
Barberry Blossoms, Showing the Approach of the Bee. Fig. 2	228
Initial. A Woolly Flock	230
One of the Flock Magnified	233
A Winged Aphis	235
Initial. Woodbine Branch and Sphinx Caterpillar	238
What Happened the Next Day	241
What He Should Have Become	244
The Mischief-Maker	245
Initial. Bearing Off the Prey	246
A Section of the Sand-bank	252
In the Dungeon	255

EYE SPY

A Naturalist's Boyhood

I AM enjoying a book, a picture, a statue, or, say, a piece of music. I know these to be the finished works of the man or the woman, but I invariably hark back to the boy or the girl.

What I want to discover is the precise time, in the lives of certain boys and girls, when the steel first struck the flint, the spark flew, and out streamed that jet of fire which never afterwards was extinguished.

I was reading an article entitled "Professor Wriggler," written by Mr. William Hamilton Gibson, which appeared in "Harper's Young People," in the number of October 31, 1893. I need not tell you that both old and young, at home and abroad, delight in reading what Mr. Hamilton Gibson has written, because he was not alone the most observant of naturalists, but a distinguished artist and a sympathetic author.

He thus filled a peculiar position in the literary and artistic world which is seldom given to any one man to fill. Besides being a naturalist from his boyhood, he was able to write better than most people what he wished to write, and to illustrate his articles in a way that was unique. Mr. Gibson's death a few days ago, therefore, has closed the career of a man who had the ability to interest a large number of people not only in natural history, but in art and literature.

The news of Mr. Gibson's death came to me suddenly, and as I was reading it I recalled an interesting talk I had with him less than a year ago about his work early in life and the way he got his start. I had been reading one of his articles to a lady, who, when she heard the name of the author, said:

"Why, I knew Mr. Hamilton Gibson long ago. When he was a lad he painted a lovely drop-curtain for us. He could not have been more than fifteen or sixteen then."

The next time I met Mr. Hamilton Gibson I asked him about this drop-curtain. "Do you remember it?"

"Certainly I do. We had a temperance society at Sandy Hook, Connecticut, and we gave a grand entertainment. I made the drop-curtain. It represented a wood. There was a rock in the foreground, and a Virginia-creeper was climbing over it."

"Was it an original composition?" I asked.

"I made many studies of the rock and the Virginia-creeper from nature. On the other side of the curtain I painted a drawing-room. There were a marble mantelpiece, a clock, and lace curtains. I don't think I enjoyed painting the clock as much as the Virginia-creeper."

"To paint a drop-curtain at fifteen or sixteen means that you had then a certain facility. But that could not have been your beginning. When did you break your shell? What chipped or cracked your egg so that your particular bird emerged, chirped, and finally took flight? That was what I wanted to know."

"Is that what you are after?" asked Mr. Hamilton

Gibson. "From my baby days I was curious about flowers and insects. The two were always united in my mind. What could not have been more than a childish guess was confirmed in my later days." Then Mr. Hamilton Gibson paused. I could see he was recalling, not without emotion, some memories of the long past.

"I was very young, and playing in the woods. I tossed over the fallen leaves, when I came across a chrysalis. There was nothing remarkable in that, for I knew what it was. But, wonderful to relate—providentially I deem it—as I held the object in my hand a butterfly slowly emerged, then fluttered in my fingers."

"You were pleased with its beauty," I said.

"Oh! It was more than that. I do not know whether I was or was not a youngster with an imagination, but suddenly the spiritual view of a new or of another life struck me. I saw in this jewel born from an unadorned casket some inkling of immortality. Yes, that butterfly breaking from its chrysalis in my hand shaped my future career."

"But some young people may feel passing impulses, but how account for your artistic skill and literary powers?"

"As to the art side, at least deftness of hand came early. I had the most methodical of grandmothers. Every day I had a certain task. I made a square of patch-work for a quilt. I learned how to sew, and I can sew neatly to-day. I knew how to use my fingers."

"Did you like patch-work?" I inquired.

"I simply despised it. Sewing must have helped me, for it was eye-training, and when I went to work with a pencil and a paint-brush I really had no trouble. I read a great deal. I devoured Cooper's novels and the Rollo series; but there was one special volume, "Harris on

Insects," I never tired of. I studied that over and over again. It was the illustrations of Marsh which fascinated me. I never found a bug, caterpillar, or butterfly that I did not compare my specimens with the Marsh pictures. I learned this way much which I have never forgotten."

"Had you any particular advantages?"

"Yes; my brother was a doctor, and he let me use his microscope, and so I acquired a knowledge of the details of flowers and insects that escape the naked eye. I pulled flowers to pieces, but not in the spirit of destruction, but so that I might better understand their structure. When I was ten I had a long illness. When I was getting better I was permitted to take an hour's or so turn in the garden. That hour I devoted to collecting insects and flowers. On my return to my room, what I had collected amused me until I could get out again next day or the day after."

"It was pleasure and study combined," I said.

"I was not conscious that I was studying. Then in my sick-room I began to draw and paint the insects. I think I was conscientious about it, and careful—perhaps minutely so. I tried to put on paper exactly what I saw, and nothing else. You say you like 'Professor Wriggler.' I drew him when I was ten or eleven, and I could not make him any more accurate to-day than I did thirty years ago."

"Were you encouraged at your work?" I inquired.

"Yes; once I was much pleased. I came across a curious insect. I could not find it in the books. I made a drawing of it and sent it to a professor of the Smithsonian, asking him to give me its scientific name. Back came by return mail my sketch, and under it the

Latin name. The professor wrote me that if the people who were always annoying him with pictures of impossible bugs would only send him as accurate a picture as was mine, he never would have any more bother."

"Did you have any setbacks?"

"Yes; and I haven't forgotten it up to to-day. I was always collecting, and I had brought together every insect I had found in my neighborhood. As I took them home I pinned them in the drawers of an old-fashioned bureau. In time the whole of the drawers, bottom and sides, were full of pinned specimens, and there was room for no more. I had saved enough money to buy a cabinet, and I went to New York and purchased one. When I returned home the first thing I did was to look at my precious collection. When I opened a drawer there was a confused mass of wings only. One single wretch of a black ant had got in, and had passed the word to 10,000 other black ants. They had eaten the bodies of my insects in all the drawers. That quite broke my heart."

"But your writing. How did that come about?" I asked.

"I don't think that you can develop in one direction only. You must unbosom yourself. You are forced to tell or to write about the things you have most at heart. When I was a small boy I wrote a book for myself, and called it 'Botany on the Half-shell.' The first thing I ever wrote which was printed was an article for one of Messrs. Harper's publications, and I made the pictures for it. That was my début."

"Then your work went hand in hand?"

"Certainly. The one was the stimulant of the other. We all grew up together. The days spent in my room when I was ill helped me. I think I studied flowers then, so that their forms and colors were indelibly impressed on my mind. When I was older I made a small bunch of flowers in wax. Not a detail escaped me. I made moulds of all kinds of leaves. Once I put together a rose, some sprigs of mignonette and heliotrope in wax, and gave them to my dear old friend, Henry Ward Beecher. He was delighted with my flowers, and put them on his study table. Presently Mrs. Beecher came in. She ran to the flowers and broke the rose all to pieces."

"How could she have done that?" I asked.

"It must have been with her nose. She wanted to smell the rose."

Then Mr. Hamilton Gibson showed me some monster drawings of flowers—Brobdingnagian ones. The flowers opened and closed when you pulled a string, showing their interior structure. Here were bees or other insects, and they flew into the flowers, collected the honey, and, above all, the pollen, and buzzed out again. He explained to me how plant life would perish if it were not for certain insects, which bring a new existence to flowers; for without these winged helpers there would be no longer any varieties of flowers or seeds.

You will see, then, that in tracing the beginning of Mr. Hamilton Gibson's career what I mean by harking backward.

I am certain, too, that in every boy and girl there is something good and excellent. Like the flower visited by the bee, all it wants is impulse. Then, as Mr. Hamilton Gibson explained it to me, will come the blossoming, and lastly perfect fruitage.

BARNET PHILLIPS.

The Story of the Floundering Beetle

AMONG my somewhat numerous correspondence from young people, I recall several wondering inquiries about a certain fat, floundering "beetle," as "blue as indigo"; and when we consider how many other observing youngsters, including youngsters of larger growth, have looked upon this uncouth shape in the path, lawn, or pasture, will speculate as to its life history, it is perhaps well to make this floundering blue beetle better acquainted with his unappreciative neighbors.

What are the lazy blue insects doing down there in the grass, for there are usually a small family of them. With the exception of their tinselled indigo-blue coat, there is certainly very little to admire in them. But what they lack in beauty they make up for in other ways. There are many of their handsomer cousins whose history is not half as interesting as that of this poor beetle that we tread upon in the grass. His neighbor insect, the tiger-beetle, running hither and thither with legs of wonderful speed, and with the agility of a fly on the wing, readily escapes our approach; but this clumsy, helpless blue beetle must needs plead for mercy by his color alone, because he has no means to avert our crushing step. A little girl who met me on the country road recently summed up the characteristics of the blue beetle pretty well. The portrait was unmistakable. "I've got a funny blue bug at home in a box that I want to show you," said she; "he's blue and awful fat, and hasn't got any wings, but when you touch him, he just turns over on his back, and trembles his toes and leaks big yellow drops out of his elbows." I have shown her beetle—three views of him, in fact—about the natural size, one of them on his back and "leaking" at his elbows, for such is the infallible habit of the insect when disturbed—a trick which has also given him the name of the "oil beetle." He is also known as the indigo beetle.

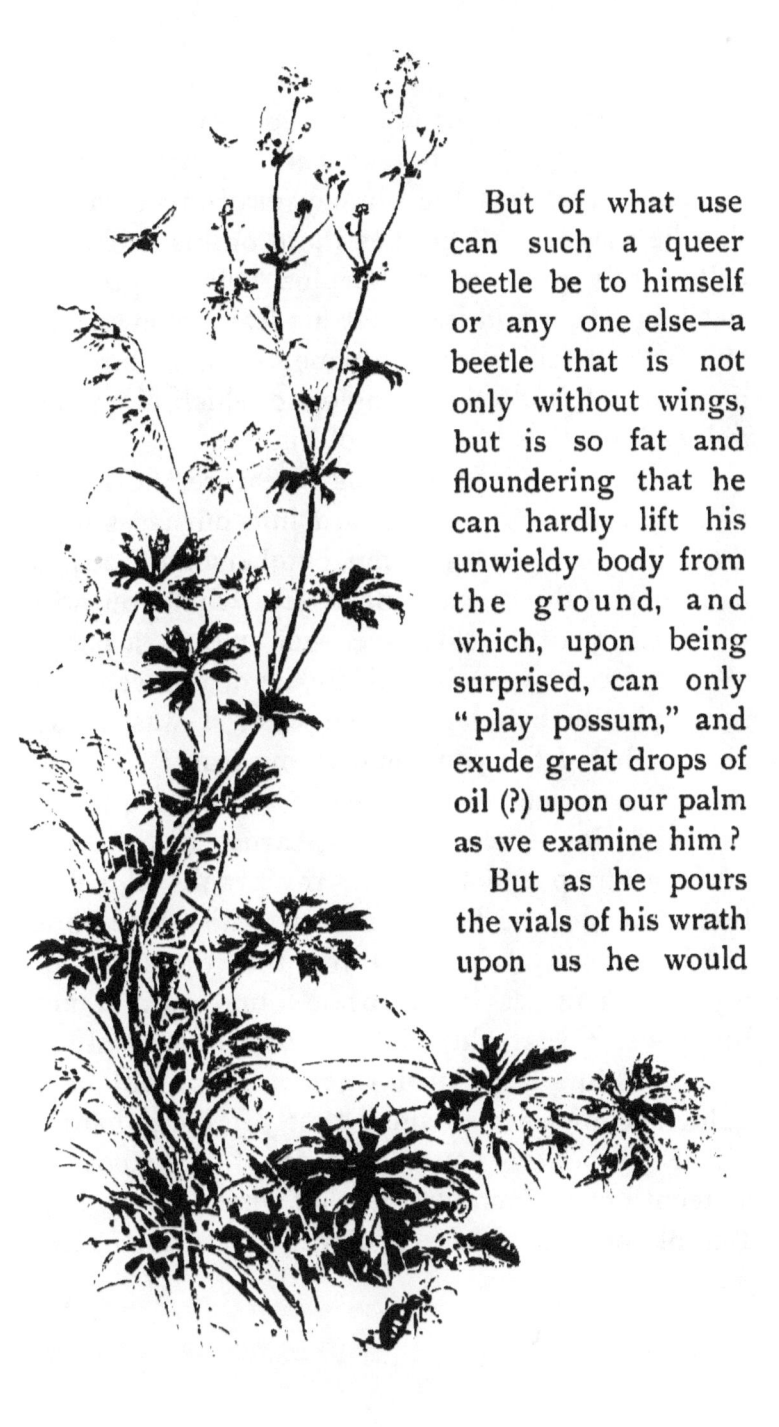

But of what use can such a queer beetle be to himself or any one else—a beetle that is not only without wings, but is so fat and floundering that he can hardly lift his unwieldy body from the ground, and which, upon being surprised, can only "play possum," and exude great drops of oil (?) upon our palm as we examine him?

But as he pours the vials of his wrath upon us he would

doubtless fain have us understand that he was not always thus unable to take care of himself, that he was not always the clumsy, crawling creature that he now is. As he lies there on his back, the yellow, oily globules of surplus "elbow grease" swelling larger and larger at his leaky elbows, and one by one falling on the paper beneath him, we may almost fancy the monologue which might be going on in that blue head of his.

"Yes, I am indeed a clumsy creature," he might be saying, as he stares upward into our faces with fixed indigo eyes, "and my cumbersome body is a burden. But I was not always what you now see. Ah, you should have seen me as a baby! Was there ever such a lively, acrobatic, venturesome, plucky baby as I, even when I was a day old? Shall I tell you some of my feats? Everybody knows me as I am *now;* but I have taken care that few shall learn my earlier history. It takes a sharp eye to follow my pranks of babyhood, and no one has been smart enough to do it yet, but I will at least let you into the secret of my life as far as it has been found out. I am little over a year old. I was born under a stone in a meadow last April, when I crept out of a golden-yellow case so small that you could hardly see it. I believe your books say I was about a sixteenth of an inch long at that time. Ah! when I think of what I *was* and what I *could do then*, and look at what I am *now*, I sometimes wonder whether that lively babyhood of mine has not all been a mocking dream.

"Do you wonder that I am as blue as indigo, and am occasionally forced to resort to my oil-tank to still the troubled waters of my later experience? Well, as I was saying (pardon this fresh display of tears), when I crept out of that filmy egg-sac I was just ready for anything, and spoiling for adventure. I found myself with a slender, agile body of thirteen joints, and three pairs of the sprightliest, spider-like legs you ever saw, each tipped with three little sharp claws. Now I knew that these long legs and claws were not given to me at this early babyhood for nothing, so I looked about for something to try them on. I had not a great while to wait, for as I crept along through the grass roots beneath the edge of the stone, I heard a welcome sound, which is music to all babies of my kind. I remembered having heard the same music in my dreams while inside the little yellow case, but now it seemed louder than ever, and in another minute I was almost blown off my feet by the breeze which the noise made, and a great black, hairy giant, as big as a house, pounced down just outside the stone. He had a great black head, and six enormous legs as big round as trees. Think how a bumblebee would look to a wee baby not half as big as a hyphen in one of your books! Did I run when I saw him coming? Not a bit of it. I just waited until he came close to me, and then I jumped on his back, and put those eighteen little claws of mine to good use as I crept over his great spiny body, and finally found a snug resting-place beneath it. And then I waited, clinging tightly with my clutching feet. In another moment I had begun to take my first outing; and did ever baby have such a ride, and to such music! After the bumblebee had remained under the stone a little while he turned and went

out again. No sooner did he get to the edge than he spread his great buzzing wings, and away we went over the world, higher and higher, miles high, over big oceans and mountains. I could see them all beneath me as I clung to the underside of the bee. I believe I must finally have got dizzy and faint, for I remember at last finding myself at rest in a queer thicket of greenish poles with big yellow balls at the top of them, and great giant leaves fringed with long, glistening hairs. They told me afterwards it was a willow blossom.

"It seemed a very good place to rest, so I dropped off from my bee and remained. Everywhere about me, as I looked, the air was yellow with these blossoms, and full of the wing-music of the bees. But, as I have said, I was a restless baby, and having had a taste of travel I soon tired of this idle life, and began to get ready for another ride. My chance soon came. This time it was a honey-bee. She alighted in the flower next to mine, but I quietly piled over and clutched upon her leg, and was soon snugly tucked away under her body, with my flat head between its segments. And now for the first time I began to feel hungry; and what was more natural than to take a bite from the tender flesh of this bee, so easily available? I did it, and liked it so well that I adopted this bee for my mother for quite a long while, taking many, many long rides every day, and always coming back to the prettiest little house on a bench under the trees. This was a sort of bee hotel, with many hundreds of guests. It was all partitioned off inside into little six-sided rooms, and the walls were so thin that you could see through them. Indeed, I soon came to like this little home so well that one morning I decided that I would not leave it again. I had begun to get tired of my roving life. I saw a lot of little white fat babies tucked away in some of these little rooms, and this very bee which I had adopted as my mother was engaged in bringing food to some of these babies and sealing them up in their nests. This was enough for me. I concluded to bring my roving habit to a close, and become a bee baby in truth; so watching for my opportunity, I loosened my clutch upon the mother bee, and dropped into one of the little rooms.

"Then I became sleepy, and can tell you nothing more than that when I woke up I didn't know who or what I was. My six spider legs had gone, and I had a half-dozen little short feet instead; and instead of the sprightly ideas of my baby days, the thought of such a thing as even moving was a bore. But I was hungrier than ever, and the first thing I did was to fall upon another fat youngster who disputed the room with me, and make short work of him. That was breakfast.

When dinner-time came, I found it right at my mouth. That busy mother of mine had fully supplied my wants, and packed my room full to the ceiling with the most delicious, fragrant bread of flowers made of pollen and honey.

"Oh, those were good old times, with all I wanted to eat all the time, and everything I ate turning to appetite! Too soon, too soon I found myself getting drowsy again, and, I can only remember awakening from a queer dream, to find even my six tiny legs gone, and, what is *worse*, my *mouth* also. While wondering and hoping that this was but a troubled vision, I was plunged into sleep again, and dreamed that I was locked up in a mummy-case for over a week. And now comes the end, the cycle of my story. From this nightmare mummy-case I finally awoke — awoke, and emerged as you now see me. Do you wonder that I have had the blues ever since at the memory of those honeyed days, now forever fled? Instead of sporting aloft in airy skyward flights, I am now a miserable groundling. Instead of sweet, fragrant bread of flowers, I am now forced to break my fast on acrid buttercup leaves. But I shall live again, with joys several hundred times multiplied, live again in my children, for whose jolly time in the autumn I shall soon lay my plans—golden promises—here in the ground beneath the buttercup leaves, close to a burrow where lives a burly bumblebee.

"But I have not told you all of my history, and will leave you to fill in the blank spaces, even as some of the scientists have to do."

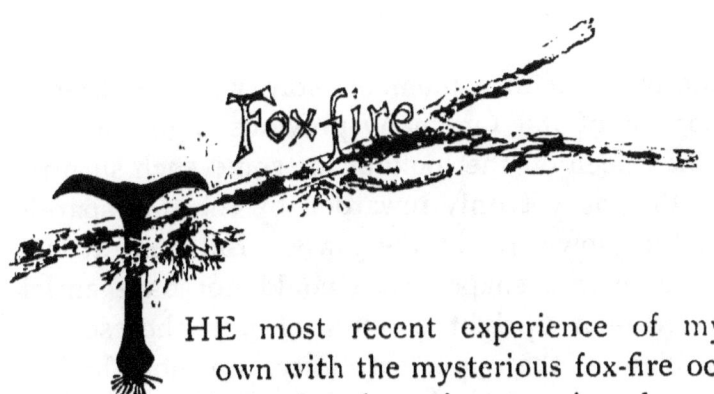

Fox-fire

THE most recent experience of my own with the mysterious fox-fire occurred a short time ago in a homeward drive with a companion from a botanizing expedition about twelve miles distant. It was near ten o'clock. The sky was overcast, only a stray star of the first magnitude now and then peeping out from between the rifts of hazy floating clouds. The new moon, "wi' th' auld moon i' her arm," had sunk below the western hills, and so dark had it become that the road ahead, at best but a faint suggestion, was occasionally lost for minutes together in the deepened gloom of the overhanging trees, only the keener nocturnal vision of the trusted horse affording the slightest hope of keeping in the wheel-tracks.

In one of these dark passages we were suddenly surprised by a gleam of light a few rods ahead to the left, and in a moment more we were directly abreast of it. On many previous night-journeys I had been on the lookout for some such surprise as this, as yet only rewarded by the tiny sparkle of the glowworm in the grass. But here, at last, it came in a shape that I could not have anticipated—an upright column of phosphorescence, brilliant at the upper extremity, and more broken below for a space of several feet. The brilliancy of the light may be inferred from the following query and its answer:

"What is that light yonder?" I asked my companion.

"A lantern reflected in water," was his reply.

The mass of light shone verily like a lantern, and the present interpretation was somewhat reminiscent of a previous flickering lantern which we had seen, with its accompaniment of great magnified moving shadows on barn and hay-stack, as it assisted in the tardy chores of a whistling farmer lad.

But this light was of a greenish, ghostly hue, and perfectly motionless, and had withal a certain weird, uncanny glare, which belongs alone to foxfire. It was impossible to locate its distance from us. It might as easily be one rod as five. I concluded to investigate its source, and, groping my way through the dewy bushes, soon confronted it. It seemed to glow with added brilliancy as I approached it, and as I stood face to face within a few inches of it no vestige of material surface appeared to sustain it; it seemed hanging motionless in mid-air. I reached out my hand, which momentarily intervened like a black silhouette

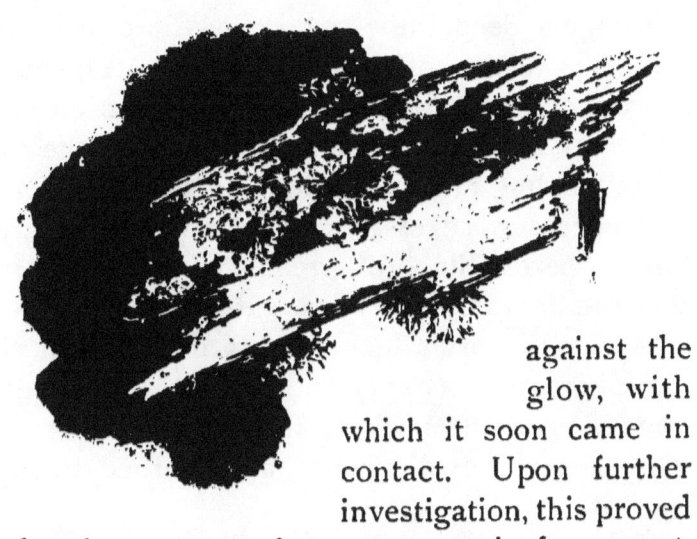

against the glow, with which it soon came in contact. Upon further investigation, this proved to be the contact of a mere prosaic fence-post, which, for some mysterious reason, had been singled out for glorification among the ten thousand others of its neighbors and transformed into a pillar of fire. The post was about six inches in diameter, its summit an unbroken mass of light, which extended in more or less broken patches below for a distance of six feet, thus suggesting the effect of the rippling elongated reflection of a lantern in water noticed by my companion, and which would doubtless have been so accepted by the average passing observer without further thought.

The most luminous upper portions were free from bark, the exposed patches of wood below being equally brilliant. Clutching at the more available part of the post, I was enabled to sink my fingers deep into its decayed fibre, and succeeded in tearing off a long fragment. The outer surface of this particular piece had been covered with bark and not especially brilliant, but the cavity of yielding moist fibre thus exposed, as well as the inner surface of the dislodged piece, poured forth a perfect flood of greenish light, indicating that the damp uncanny fire extended to the very core of the post, which was saturated with the phosphorescent essence. I laid this and other fragments in the back of the carriage, where its glare met our eyes whenever we turned to look upon it.

Taking it beneath the lamp-light upon our return home, it resolved itself into a very ordinary piece of yellowish rotten wood. In a more shaded corner of the room it appeared as though whitewashed, and upon taking it into a closet or out into the night again its flame gradually rekindled, as though feeding upon the darkness, until it appeared precisely as when we found it.

By enclosing the specimen in a tin box with moist moss I was enabled to prolong the effulgence until the next evening, but it had entirely disappeared by the following night, at which time its original haunt, the post, was also doubtless lost in the darkness. A week later I again passed its neighborhood in the late hours without the slightest hint of its presence.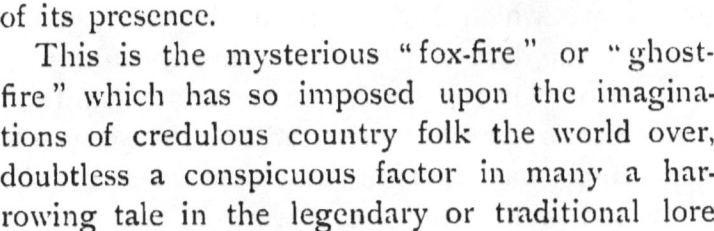

This is the mysterious "fox-fire" or "ghost-fire" which has so imposed upon the imaginations of credulous country folk the world over, doubtless a conspicuous factor in many a harrowing tale in the legendary or traditional lore of spooks and goblins.

I remember the breathless interest with which as a boy I listened to the weird story, whose scene was located not far from my native town, of a ghostly light that flickered about the eaves of a certain old ruin of a house in the neighborhood, and also above the well close by in the weedy waste of the former door-yard.

The light was seen by many for several consecutive nights. It fairly glowed into a halo up from the wooden curb which surmounted the well, where it was viewed at a safe distance with bated breath by a curious crowd of villagers, not one of whom would have dared to steal up and surprise the innocent spook in its haunt—doubtless a mass of fox-fire which had found its brief, congenial home in the decaying boards within the tottering well-curb. Of course the house was "haunted" for evermore, and rustic tradition for a whole generation was rich in fabulous tales of the "haunted well," and there was serious talk of unearthing the nameless mystery which lay at the bottom of it.

A certain saw-mill was also tenanted by a similar luminous ghost one night after a heavy rain, but the shape of the spook in this case was so peculiar, and so exactly corresponded with the parallel cross-boxes of the old broken water-wheel, that it was considered harmless.

But it is scarcely to be wondered at that a phenomenon so startling and inexplicable to the rustic mind should be associated with the supernatural. One's first experience with fox-fire, especially if

he chances upon a specimen of some size, is apt to be a memorable incident.

My own first encounter dates back to the age of about eight years. While walking through a wood at night I chanced upon what I supposed to be a large glowworm in my path. I picked it up, only to find in my hand a hard piece of dead twig.

A later experience, which, while quite startling for a moment, was robbed of its full terrors by the reminiscence of the first. As in the former case, I was returning home at night through a dark, damp wood. I was skirting the border of a small runnel, when I was suddenly brought to a breathless standstill, apparently confronted by the glaring eyes of a panther, or perhaps a tiger; certainly no cat or fox or owl was possessed of eyes of such dimensions or wide interspace as those which glared at me from the dark shadow of yonder copse. But in a moment my quickened pulse had subsided, and I calmly returned the greenish phosphorescent gaze, observing that a singular accident had re-enforced the first illusion by a wonderful semblance to ears and outline of body, in keeping with the formidable eyes.

In a moment I was attacking the foe, my hands stroking his rough barky forehead, and my fingers penetrating his eyes, which proved to be two holes in the bark of a fallen log, the farther side of which disclosed a brilliant, luminous patch which, as I invaded it with my hand, proved to be bare, exposed wood. Taking hold of the loose bark, a vigorous pull dislodged a great piece some three feet long, at the same time liberating a glare of greenish light from the exposed surface of the log, which was responded to in sympathy by the inner surface of the slab of bark in my hands, in all representing about six square feet of brilliant phosphorescence.

I carried a fragment home, and upon inspecting it by lamp-light, found it white with thready mould, resembling the so-called "dry-rot" of mouldy timber — doubtless the mother of some well-known fungus, or "toadstool," which might have been discerned upon the log the following day had I chanced thither.

Hawthorne in one of his books records a remarkable personal encounter with this weird fox-fire, and one which cost him dearly. He was on a journey by canal-boat, which had stopped *en route* for a brief period at midnight. During the interval he had stepped ashore, and was decoyed into a neighboring wood by the bright glow, which proved to be a fallen tree ablaze with phosphorescence.

In his surprise and interest he lost all account of time, and thus missed his boat, and was obliged to "foot it" for miles on the midnight tow-path, which he was enabled to do by the aid of a big brand of the tree which he used as a flambeau.

Almost any damp wood, especially after a rain, is likely to disclose its fox-fire, but it occasionally appears under circumstances where we little expect it. A few weeks since, having occasion to go to my refrigerator after dark, I noticed a brilliant glowing object upon the floor beneath it, which I found upon inspection to be merely a piece of damp bread. Can it be that the yeast fungus too may give off effulgence with its carbonic acid at its whim? or was the light traceable to the perceptible odor of lobster with which it had evidently been previously in contact?

Dead fish are frequently thus luminous, and brilliant phosphorescence is often an accompaniment of decomposition of both animal and vegetable matter. A few decaying potatoes will often light up a corner of a cellar which is dim by daylight, and an instance is on record of a certain cellar full of these vegetables giving off such a flood of light as to lead observers to suppose that the premises were on fire.

Many animals, and especially fishes and insects, possess luminous properties. The familiar examples of the glowworm and fire-fly hardly need be mentioned. Then there are the big lantern-flies, with their luminous heads; and brilliant snapping beetles of the South, with their two glowing headlights, so effectively employed as ornaments for the hair and otherwise in the toilet of the Cuban belle. But the sea is the home of luminous life. From the diminutive myriads of the *noctiluca*, which sets the sea aflame, to the numerous larger finny tribes, the ocean is peopled with animal life, which, though dwelling in depths scarce reached by the faintest gleam from the sun, swim about enveloped in their self-illumined halo.

While all these phenomena come under the general term of phosphorescence, the inference of the presence of phosphorus is incorrect; many substances without a trace of phosphorus in their constitution emit light with equal brilliancy.

The well-known commercial article called "luminous paint" is an apt example, which, while containing no trace of phosphorus, glows like fox-fire at night, especially after having been exposed to the sun's rays during the day, giving forth in the dark hours the light which it has thus absorbed, and being thus of utility in its application to clock faces and match-boxes.

Calcined lime and burnt oyster-shells, in combination with certain acids, become luminous at night by the similar power of absorption and transmission of light vibration which is supposed to be the secret of much of the so-called phosphorescence.

But fox-fire is believed to be of a different nature, more chemical in its character, and usually emanates from a fungus, either visible in the form of mould or toadstool, or existing as an almost invisible essence which saturates the decaying wood, a species known as *Thelaphora cerulea* being credited with most of the luminous manifestations.

Fox-fire is occasionally put to a cruel utility by hunters in association with the "salt-lick" for deer. Salt is scattered in a selected spot, and a piece of fox-fire adjusted beyond it in direct line of the aim of the rifle, which is securely fixed in place. The sudden obscuration of the light is a sufficient signal for the still-hunter, who has only to pull the trigger to secure the game, even though the latter be entirely hid in the darkness.

The more common examples of fox-fire are small bits of decayed wood, but most astonishing specimens have been observed. In addition to the fine example mentioned by Hawthorne, there is an authentic record of a single log twenty-four feet in length and a foot in diameter which was one mass of brilliant phosphorescence.

A Homely Weed

with

Interesting Flowers

THE recent article from my pen on the "Riddle of the Bluets," and which showed the important significance of its two forms of blossoms, suggests that a few more similar expositions of the beautiful mysteries of the common flowers which we meet every day in our walks, and which we claim to "know" so well, may serve to add something to the interest of our strolls afield. It is scarcely fair to assert that familiarity can breed contempt in our relations to so lovely an object as a flower, but certain it is that this every-day contact or association, especially with the wild things of the wood, meadow, and way-side, is conducive to an apathy which dulls our sense to their actual attributes of beauty. Many of these commonplace familiars of the copse and thicket and field are indeed like voices in the wilderness to most of us. We forget that the "weed" of one country often becomes a horticultural prize in another, even as the mullein, for which it is hard for the average American to get up any enthusiasm, and which is tolerated with us only in a worthless sheep pasture, flourishes in distinction in many an English or Continental garden as the "American velvet plant."

The extent of our admiration often depends upon the relative rarity of the flower rather than upon its actual claims to our appreciation. The daisy which whitens our meadows — the "pesky white-weed" of the farmer—we are perfectly willing to see in the windrows of the scythe or tossed in the air by the fork of the hay-maker. The meed of our appreciation of the single blossom becomes extremely thin when spread over a ten-acre lot. How rarely do we see a bouquet of daisies on a country table? And yet, strange inconsistency! the marguerite of our goodwife's window-garden, almost identical with the daisy and not one whit prettier, is a prize, because it came from the "florist's," and cost twenty-five cents, with five cents extra for the pot.

A certain thrifty granger of the writer's acquaintance was recently converted from the error of his attitude towards the "tarnal weeds and brush." He was one of the tribe of blind, misguided vandals who had always deemed it his first duty "after hayin'" to invade with his scythe all the adjacent roadside, to "tidy things up," reducing to most unsightly untidiness that glorious wild garden of August's floral cornucopia, that luxuriant tangle of purple eupatorium, the early asters, golden-rod, vervains, wild-carrot, and meadow-rue.

He was converted in the sanctuary, where one August Sabbath he beheld by the side of the pulpit, dignified by a large, beautiful vase, a great bouquet of this very tall, purple thoroughwort, meadow-rue, and wild-carrot of his abomination, and which had actually fallen before his scythe on the evening previous. "Well, there!" he exclaimed; "I didn't realize they *was* so pretty!"

The beauty of the commonplace often requires the aid of the artist as its interpreter, a fact which Browning realized when he expressed, through Fra Lippo Lippi:

"We're made so that we love
First when we see them painted, things which we have passed
Perhaps a hundred times, nor cared to see."

An illustration of the truth of this axiom was afforded in a recent incident in my experience. Sitting at the open window of my country studio one summer day, engaged in making a portrait of a common weed, a friendly farmer, chancing "across lots," seeing me at work, sauntered up to "pass the time o' day." As he leaned on the window-sill his eye fell upon the drawing before me.

"My!" he exclaimed, "but ain't that pooty?"

"What!" I retorted, "and will *you admit* that this drawing of a *weed* is pretty?"

"Yes, your *draft* thar is pooty, but you artist fellows alliz makes 'em look pootier 'n they *ought* to."

So much for the mere attributes of manifest outward beauty without regard to consideration of "botany" or the structural beauty of the flowers. The "botanist" finds beauty everywhere, even among the homeliest of Flora's hosts. But in the light of the "new botany," which recognizes the insect as the important affinity of the flower—the key to its various puzzling features of color, form, and fragrance—every commonest blossom which we thought we had "known" all our lives, and every homely weed scarce worth our knowing, now becomes a rebuke, and offers us a field of investigation as fresh and promising as is offered by the veriest rare exotic of the conservatory;

more so, indeed, because these latter are strangers in a strange land, and divorced from their ordained insect affinities. The plebeian daisy now becomes a marvel of a flower indeed—five hundred wonderful little mechanisms packed together in a single golden disk. The red clover refuses to recognize us now unless properly introduced by that "burly bumblebee" with which its life is so strangely linked.

The barn-yard weeds need no longer be considered uninteresting and commonplace, because their mysteries have not yet been discovered, and I can do no better in my present chapter than to select one of their number and redeem it from its hitherto lowly place among them—one of the homeliest of them all, and whose blossoms are scarce noticed by any one except a botanist.

In my initial illustration is shown a sketch of the Figwort, or scrophularia, a tall, spindling weed, with rather fine, luxuriant leaves, it is true, but with a tall, curiously branching spray of small, insignificant purplish-olive flowers, with not even a perfume, like the mignonette, to atone for its plainness. But it has an *odor* if not a perfume, and it has a nectary which secretes the beads of sweets for its pet companion insects, which in this instance do not happen to be bees or butterflies, but most generally wasps of various kinds, as

A. First Day's Welcome—
Stigma at the Doorway.

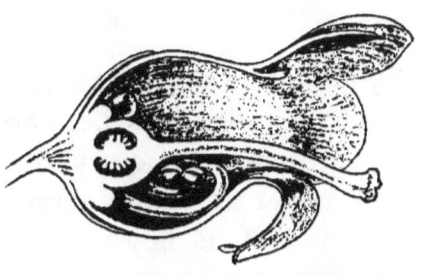

A¹. First Day—Sectional View.

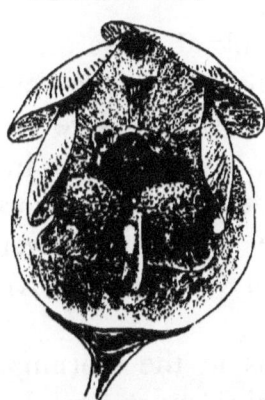

B. Second Day's Welcome.—Stigma bent downward beneath two withered Stamens at Doorway.

B¹. Second Day—Sectional View.

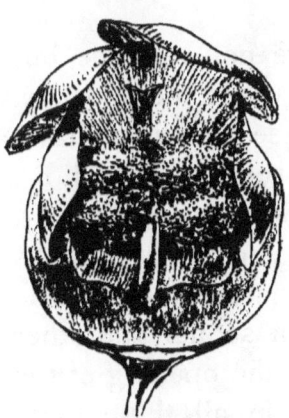

C. Third Day's Welcome.—Four Stamens at Doorway.

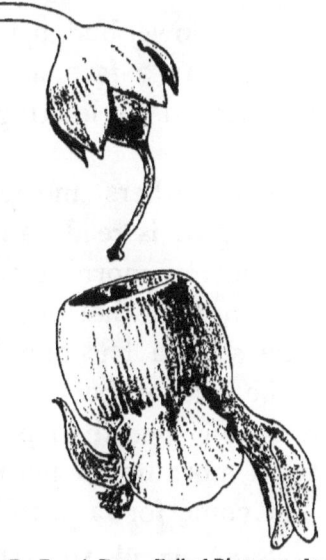

D. Fourth Day.—Full of Blossom. Its Mission fulfilled.

these insects are not so particular as to the quality of their tipple as bees are apt to be. But the figwort has found out gradually through the ages that *wasps* are more serviceable in the cross-fertilization of its flowers than other insects, and it has thus gradually modified its shape, odor, and nectar especially to these insects.

Let us then take a careful look at these queer little homely flowers, and for the time being consider them as mere devices — first, to insure the visit of an insect, and, second, to make that insect the bearer of the pollen from one blossom to the stigma of another. Here we see a flower with three distinct welcomes on three successive days.

The flower-bud usually opens in the morning, and shows a face as at A, which must be fully understood by looking at the side section shown at A'.

The anthers and pollen are not yet ripe, but the stigma is ready, and now guards the doorway. To-morrow morning we shall see a new condition of things at that doorway, as seen at B and B'. The stigma has now bent down out of the way, while two anthers have unfolded on their stalks and now shed their pollen at the threshold. The third morning, or perhaps even sooner, the other pair come forward, and we see the opening of the blossom as at C. Blossoms in all these three conditions are to be found on this cluster.

A small wasp is now seen hovering about the flowers, and we must turn our attention to him as seen in Figs. 1, 2, and 3. The insect alights, we will assume, on a blossom of the second day (Fig. 1), clinging with all his feet, and thrusting his tongue into the beads of nectar shown at A' and B'. He now brings his breast or thorax, or perhaps the underside of his head, against the pollen, and is thoroughly dusted with it. Leaving the blossom, we see him in flight, as at Fig. 2, and very soon he is seen to come to a freshly opened flower, which he sips as before. The pollen is thus pushed against the projecting stigma, as shown at Fig. 3, and thus, one by one, the flowers are cross-sterilized.

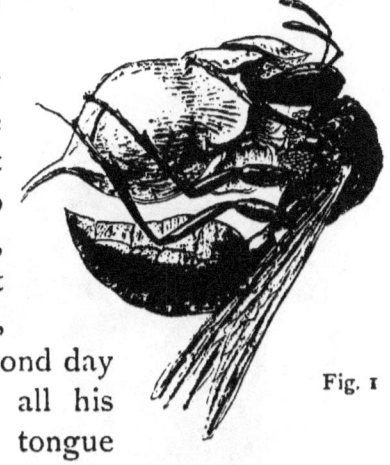

Fig. 1

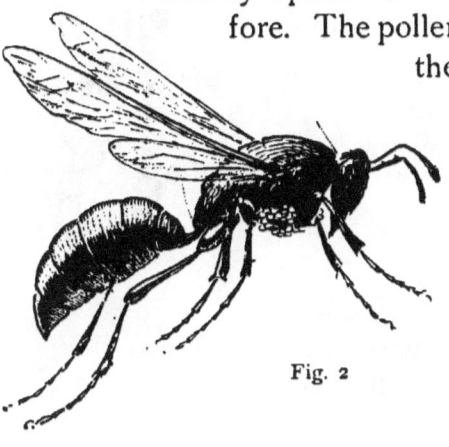

Fig. 2

The stigma, after receiving pollen, immediately bends downward and backward, as shown in B¹, to give place to the ripening anthers, and shortly after the last pair of them

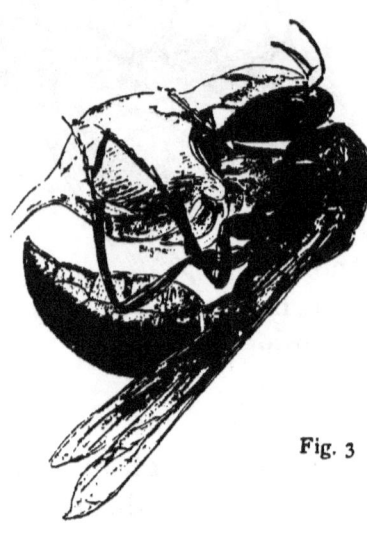

Fig. 3

have shed their pollen the blossom, having then fulfilled its functions, falls off, as shown at D. This may be on the afternoon of the third day, or not until the fourth. If not visited by insects it may chance to remain the longer time; but more than one tiny wasp gets his head into such a blossom, and is surprised with a tumble, his weight pulling the blossom from its attachment.

The result of that pollen upon the stigma is quickly seen in the growing ovary or pod, which enlarges rapidly on the few succeeding days, as in E.

Many species of hornets and wasps, large and small, are to be seen about the figwort blooms, occasionally bees, frequently bumblebees, which usually car-

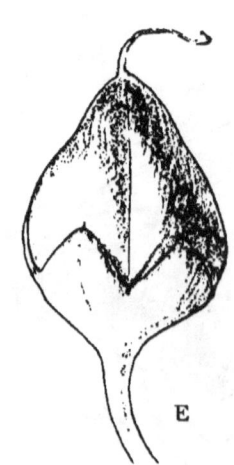

E

ry away the pollen on the underside of their heads.

Who shall any longer refer to the figwort as an "uninteresting weed"?

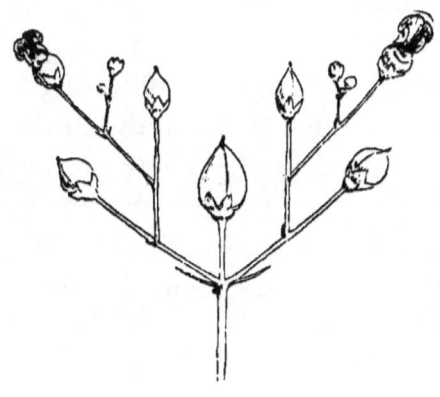

Two Fairy Sponges

THE pretty works of my fairy and his companions in mischief are seen on every hand from spring until winter, but few of us have ever seen the fay, for Puck is no myth nor Ariel a creature of the poet's fancy. Their prototype existed in entomological entity and demoralizing mischievousness ages before the traditional fay, in diminutive human form, had been dreamed of. The quaint, bow-legged little "brownies," which have brought our entire land beneath the witching spell of their drollery, can scarce claim prestige in the ingenuity of their mischief, nor can the droll doings of imps and elves chronicled in the folk-lore of many an ancient people begin to match the actual doings of the real, live, busy little fairy whose works abound in meadow, wood, and copse, and which any of us may discover if we can once be brought to realize that our imp is visible. Then we must not forget that ideal type of the true "fairy" — a paragon of beauty and goodness, with golden hair and dazzling crown of brilliants, with her airy costume of gossamer begemmed and spangled, her dainty, twinkling feet and gorgeously painted butterfly wings. And we all remember that wonderful wand which she carried so gracefully, and whose simple touch could evoke such a train of surprising consequences.

And who shall say that our pretty fay is a myth, or her magic wand a wild creation of the fancy? May we not see the wonder-workings of that potent wand on every hand, even though our fairy has eluded us while she cast the spell? There are a host of these wee fairies continually flitting about among the trees plotting all sorts of mischief and leaving an astonishing witness of their visitation in their trail as they pass from leaf to leaf or twig to twig. But these fairies, like those of Grimm and Laboulaye, are agile little atoms, and are not to be caught in their pranks if they know it, and even though our eye chanced to rest on one of them, it is doubtful whether we would recognize him, so different is the guise of these *real* fairies from those invented creatures of the books. Once, when a mere boy, I caught one of the little imps at work, and watched her for several minutes without dreaming that I had been looking at a real fairy all this time. What did I see? I was sitting in a clearing, partly in the shade of a sapling growth of oak which sprang from the trunk of a felled tree. While thus half reclining I noticed a diminutive, black, wasp-like insect upon one of the oak leaves close to my face.

The insect seemed almost stationary, and not inclined to resent my intrusion, so I observed her closely. I soon discovered that she was inserting her sting into the midstem of the leaf, or perhaps withdrawing it therefrom, for in a few moments the midge flew away. I remember wondering what the insect was trying to do, and not until years later did I realize that I had been witnessing the secret arts of the magician of the insect world—a very Puck or Ariel, as I have said—a fairy with a magic wand which any sprite in elfindom might covet.

The wand of Herrmann never wrought such a

wonder as did this magic touch of the little black fly upon the oak leaf. Had I chanced to visit the spot a few weeks later, what a beautiful red-cheeked apple could I have plucked from that hemstitched leaf!

This was but one of a veritable swarm of mischief-making midges everywhere flitting among the trees; and while they are quite as various in their shapes as the traditional forms of fairies—the ouphes and imps, the gnomes and elves of quaintest mien, as well as the dainty fays and sylphs and sprites—there is one feature common to them all which annihilates the ideal of all the pictorial authorities on fairydom. Neither Grimm, nor Laboulaye, nor any of the masters of fairy-lore, seems to have discovered that a fairy has no right to those butterfly wings which the pages of books show us. Those of the real fairy are quite different, being narrow and glassy, and bear the magician's peculiar sign in their crisscross veins.

What a world of mischief is going on here in the fields! Here is one of the witching sprites among the drooping blossoms of the oak. "You would fain be an acorn," she says, as she pierces the tender blossoms with her wand, "but I charge thee bring forth a string of currants;" and immediately the blossoms begin to obey the behest, and erelong a mimic string of currants droops upon the stem. Upon another tender branch near by a jet-black, gauze-winged elf is casting a similar spell, which is this time followed by a tiny, downy, pink-cheeked peach. And here alights a tiny sprite, whose magic touch evokes even from the *same* leaf a cherry, or a coral bead, perhaps a huge green apple! How many of us have seen the little elf that spends her life among the tangles of creeping cinque-foil, and decks its stems with those brilliant scarlet beads which we may always find upon them, looking verily like tempting berries.

We see here about us swarms of these busy elves in obedience to their own peculiar mischievous promptings. What whispers this glittering midge to the oak twig here to which she clings so closely? We may not guess; but if we pass this way a month or so hence, what a beautiful response in the glistening, rosy-clouded sponge which encircles the stem! "But this sponge is not pretty enough by half," exclaims a rival fairy. "Wait until you see what yonder sweetbrier rose will do for *me*." Hovering thither among its thorns, she imparts her spell, and, lo! within a month the stem is clothed in emerald fringe, which grows apace, until it has become a dense pompon of deep crimson — a sponge worthy the toilet of the fairy queen herself!

Who shall still say that the fairy is a myth!

These two fairy sponges are familiar to us all, at least to those of us who dwell for even a small part of the year in the country, and use our eyes. Indeed, we need go no farther than our city parks, or even our "back-yard" gardens, to find at least one of them, for the sweetbrier is rarely neglected by this particular fairy.

So many specimens of both of these sponges have been sent to me by "Round Table" correspondents and others that I have begun to wonder how many of those other young people who have seen them and kept silence have wondered at their secret.

The two fairies which are responsible for these sponges have been captured by the inquisitive scientist, and have had their portraits taken for the rogues' gallery, and now we see them stuck

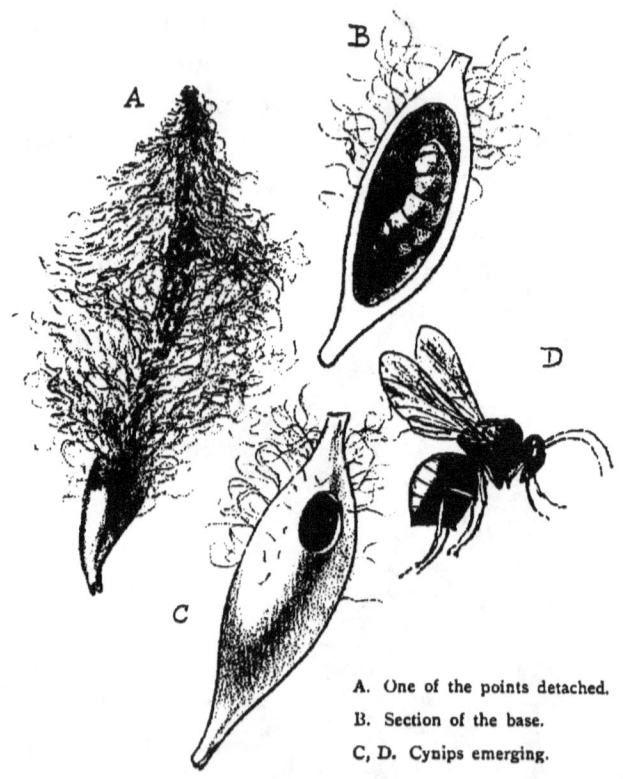

A. One of the points detached.
B. Section of the base.
C, D. Cynips emerging.

upon tiny little three-cornered pieces of paper, and pinned in the specimen case as mere *insects* —gall-flies. The one is labelled *Cynips seminator*, the other, *Cynips rosæ*.

And now the prosaic entomologist proceeds to supplant fact for fancy. This gall-fly is a sort of cousin to the wasps, but what we would call its sting is more than a mere sting. Like a sting, it seems to puncture the bark or leaf, and at the same time probably to inject its drop of venom; but at the same time it conveys to the depths of the wound a tiny egg, or perhaps a host of them. One gall-fly is thus a magician in chemistry, at least, for no sooner are these eggs deposited than the wounded branch begins to swell and form a cellular growth or tumor about them, the character of this abnormal growth depending upon the peculiar charm of the venomous touch—to one a tiny coral globe, to another a cluster of spines, to another a curved horn, and to our cynips of the white or scrub oak a peculiar globular, spongy growth which completely envelops the stem, sometimes to the size of a small apple. In its prime it is a beautiful object, with its fibrous, glistening texture studded with pink points. But this condition lasts but a few days, when the entire mass becomes brownish and woolly, which fact has given this insect the common name of "wool-sower."

And now we must lose no time if we would follow its history to its complete cycle. If we put one of these faded sponges in a tight-closed box, we shall in a few days learn the secret of its being. For this singular mimic fruit which has sprung at the behest of the gall-fly, like other fruits, has its seeds — seeds which are animated with peculiar life, and which sprout in a way we would hardly expect. Within a fortnight after gathering, perhaps, we find our box swarming with tiny, black flies, while if we dissect the sponge we find its long-beaked seeds entirely empty, and each with a clean round hole gnawed through its shell, explaining this host of gall-flies, all similar to the parent of a few weeks since, and all bent on the same mischief when you shall let them loose at the window.

The beautiful sponge of the sweet-brier has been called into being by exactly similar means, and its hard, woody centre is packed full of

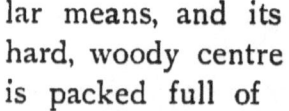

cells, at first each with its tiny egg, and then with its plump larva, followed by the chrysalis, and at length by the emergence of the full-fledged *Cynips rosæ*.

This sponge-gall of the rose is commonly known as the Bedegnar, and, like all other members of its tribe, as with the familiar oak-apple, was long supposed to be a regular accessory fruit of its parent stalk. Among early students were many superstitions connected with the Bedegnar, the nature of which may readily be inferred from its other common name of "Robin's Pin-cushion."

GREEN PANSIES

THE casual observer may perhaps have noticed that interesting law of nature which governs the coloring of flowers, and which confines the hues of a given flower, or perhaps a botanical group of flowers, to two colors and the combination of these colors. The three primary colors—red, yellow, and blue—are rarely to be seen in the blossoms of the same botanical group. Thus we observe roses, hollyhocks, chrysanthemums, and tulips in all shades of white, yellow, pink, red, and crimson, even almost approaching black, and numberless combinations of these colors, but never blue. The same is true with dahlias, zinnias, lilies, gladioli, pinks, and portulacas.

On the other hand, flowers which are notably blue—as in the bellworts, or "Canterbury-bells," and larkspur, which vary from white, through all shades of blue, to purple, pink, and even reds—never show any trace of yellow. This color limitation of blossoms was noted by De Candolle early in the present century, who classified flowers in two series as to their hues. The first, which included the yellow, was called the *Xanthic;* the second, which omitted the yellow, the *Cyanic*.

World-wide fame and a comfortable fortune await the florist who shall produce a variety of blue rose, tulip, hollyhock, or dahlia, or a yellow geranium or larkspur, which all persist in their fidelity to their particular color series. And yet nature gives us occasional exceptions which, however, only serve by their contrast to emphasize the universal law. Thus we see the water-lily group—if we include the two separate orders *Nymphæa* and *Nelumbo*—with blossoms of pink, yellow, and blue. The water-lilies of this latter color, allied to the Egyptian yellow lotus, which were to be seen in the Union Square fountain, New York, last summer, were almost lost in the azure of the sky which their surrounding waters reflected, and yet they clearly had no right to include blue in their gamut; purple or red possibly, but not blue.

But this is not so remarkable an exception as we find in the hyacinth, in which the three primary colors are to be seen with notable purity—blues, yellows, and reds—and thus with possibilities of almost any conceivable color, under cultivation and careful selection.

Another striking exception, and one which would have puzzled De Candolle for its color classification, is the columbine. One common species of the Eastern United States, *Aquilegia canadensis*, is of a pure deep scarlet color, as every country boy knows. If we seek for our columbines in the far West we shall miss this familiar type, and find it replaced by another species, *A. chrysantha*, of a fine clear yellow, or perhaps by its near relative, the *A. cœrulea*, with its sky-blue corolla, a common species in the region of the Rocky Mountains. Columbines, red, yellow, and blue, are thus to be found in a state of nature, and we thus find other cultivated forms which extend from a pure white through all shades of purple.

The pansy, that protean offspring from lowly "johnny-jumper," occasionally comes very near embracing the entire gamut of color to which its name, *Viola tricolor*, would seem to entitle it. Blue pansies and yellow pansies we certainly have, but the ruddiest of its rich wine tints, when laid beside the red, red rose, at once confesses its purple, the remnant of blue which it cannot absolutely eliminate.

The blue rose, blue tulip, blue dahlia, and blue carnation have as yet refused to respond to the coaxing arts of the florist, but he has at least succeeded in imposing upon our credulity in a carnation pink of white, streaked with peacock blue. Bouquets of these uncanny-looking blossoms are frequently to be seen in our city flower-booths, but they smack of trickery, and the vendor is rarely seen to look you in the eye as he responds "new variety" to your inquiry as to the peculiar color.

"Are those natural?" I heard a lady ask at a flower-stall recently, referring to these pinks.

"Sure, madam," he replied, this time with easy conscience. "They were picked in the conservatory this morning."

But as he folded the paper carefully about her generous purchase, he didn't trouble her with the details of the subsequent aniline bath to which they were subjected, and of which they bore plain evidence upon close scrutiny.

But if we are to resort to hocus-pocus in the

tinting of flowers, there *is* an artificial method available which leaves this clumsy artifice of the blue-green pinks far behind, and which, withal, affords a very pretty experiment in chemistry, albeit presumably more enjoyed by the operator than the victim.

A gentleman of the writer's acquaintance, while visiting his sister at her country home, noted her fondness for pansies, as indicated by the numerous beds and borders of the flowers there. After expressing his appreciation and surprise at the endless shades of color in the bouquet which she was gathering for the library table, he stooped, and apparently plucked one of the blossoms from a bed.

"Your pansies are certainly the most remarkable that I have ever seen. Here is one which is truly most astonishing in color," he remarked, as he handed the blossom to her.

It was received with an exclamation of amazement, and with eager glances at the neighborhood of the bed from which she presumed it had been taken. "Where *did* you find it?" exclaimed his sister, in complete demoralization. "Which plant was it on? Why, I never *saw* such a pansy! It's wonderful! There must be more. I never *heard* of such a pansy! Do show me where you picked it."

"I got it from this plant here, I think," replied

the young man, as soon as he could be heard; and, stooping carelessly, he plucked another, which proved even more of a surprise than the first, so vividly intense was its color.

The first specimen was a dark pansy. The two usually deep purple upper petals now appeared of a deep velvety peacock blue. The remaining three petals were pale emerald-green, bordered with deeper green. In the second blossom the upper pair of petals were now transfigured in vivid emerald-green, the rest of the flower being of paler but almost equally dazzling brilliancy.

The demoralization was more and more complete as another and another of the remarkable blossoms was rescued from its obscurity, always by the accommodating young man, and added to the growing bouquet. Neighbors on right and left were quickly acquainted with the remarkable discovery, and a gathering of excited natives soon assembled in the parlor to view the new floral sensation. The pansy-beds were soon the scene of busy commotion, but in the eager search for the rare blooms fortune seemed still to favor the young man, to the exasperation of several of the bright-eyed young ladies, who, of course, did not happen to know of the young man's occasional sly recourse to a certain tumbler concealed near by.

But the secret soon leaked out, and the victim

confessed and did penance. Had he realized what a commotion his innocent prank was destined to create, he would not have yielded to temptation. But his sister was primarily to blame. Why had she placed that bottle so conspicuously upon his wash-stand? He had noted her fondness for pansies, and a minute later had read "Ammonia" on the label of the bottle, and association of ideas and mischief did the rest. In a casual stroll about the pansy-beds he had then gathered a dozen or so of the several varieties and taken them to his room. Laying a piece of crumpled paper in a saucer, he then poured about a teaspoonful of the ammonia upon it, afterwards gently laying the pansies in a pile upon the paper, and thus free from actual contact with the liquid, and covering the whole with a tumbler. In two or three minutes the fumes of the ammoniacal gas had done their work, and lo! when he removed the tumbler his pansies had doffed their blues and purples, and were transfigured in velvets of all imaginable emerald and peacock and mineral greens, though still retaining their perfect shape and petal texture.

To more completely confound the innocent with this experiment, the "operator" should suddenly discover an entire plant with all its flowers thus tinted in emerald—a feat which may be accomplished by submitting the whole plant to similar treatment beneath a bell glass or other air-tight vessel or box, in which case the amount of ammonia used should be proportionately increased. If the *concentrated* ammonia is employed, a very small quantity will be sufficient.

Flowers thus treated

will last in an unaltered condition for several hours, though the treatment is really injurious, even destructive, to the tissues of flower as well as plant.

Various other blossoms respond in their own particular virescent hues to the vapors of ammonia, as the reader will discover upon experiment.

The fumes of sulphur confined beneath a glass, as from a few common, old-fashioned matches, will play all sorts of similar pranks with the colors of petals. A little experimenting in this direction will afford many surprises.

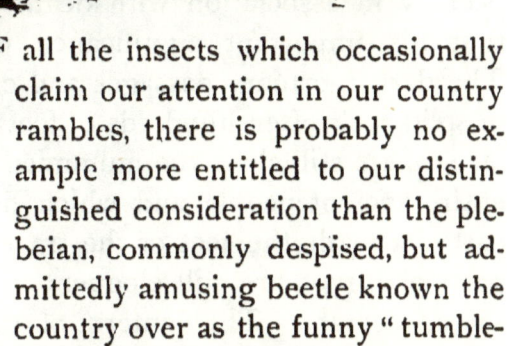
OF all the insects which occasionally claim our attention in our country rambles, there is probably no example more entitled to our distinguished consideration than the plebeian, commonly despised, but admittedly amusing beetle known the country over as the funny "tumble-bug." As we see him now, so he has always been—the same in appearance, the same in habits; yet how has he fallen from grace! how humbled in the eyes of man from that original high estate when, in ancient Egypt, he enjoyed the prestige above all insects—where, as the sacred "scarabæus," he was dignified as the emblem of immortality, and worshipped as a god! The archæological history of Egypt is rich in reminders of his former eminence. Not only do we see his familiar shape (as shown in our initial design) everywhere among

those ancient hieroglyphs engraved in the rock or pictured on the crumbling papyrus; but it is especially in association with death and the tomb that his important significance is emphasized. The dark mortuary passages and chambers hewn in solid rock, often hundreds of feet below the surface, where still sleep the mummied remains of an entire ancient people, and which honeycomb the earth beneath the feet of the traveller in certain parts of Egypt, are still eloquent in tribute to the sacred scarab. The lantern of the antiquarian explorer in those dark dungeons of death discloses the suggestive figure of this beetle everywhere engraved in high relief upon the walls, perhaps enlivened with brilliant color still as fresh as when painted three thousand years ago, emblazoned in gold and gorgeous hues upon the sarcophagus and the mummy-case within, and again upon the outer covers of the winding-sheet; finally, in the form of small ornaments the size of nature, beautifully carved on precious stones enclosed within the wrappings of the mummy itself.

What other insect has been thus glorified and immortalized? For the sake of its proud lineage, if nothing else, is not our poor tumble-bug deserving of our more than passing attention? An insect which has thus been distinguished by an entire great people of antiquity has some claims on our respect and consideration.

But aside from his historical fame, he will well repay our careful study, and serve to while away a pleasant hour in the observance of his queer habits. He is now no longer the awe-inspiring sacred scarab, but Mr. Tumble-bug, or, rather, " Mr. and Mrs. Tumble-bug," for a tumble-bug always pictured in the ancient hieroglyph is rarely to be seen in its natural haunts. Mr. and Mrs. Tumble-bug are devoted and inseparable, and, as a rule, vie with each other in the solicitude for that precious rolling ball with which the insects are always associated. From June to autumn we may find our tumble-bugs. There are a number of species included in the group of Scarabæus to which they belong. Two species are particularly familiar, one of a lustrous bronzy hue, with a very rounded back, usually found at work on the country highway in the track of the horse, and the other, the true typical tumble-bug, a flat-backed, jet-black lustrous species which we naturally associate with the barn-yard and cow-pasture. The latter may be taken as an illustrative example of his class, and his ways are identical with those of his ancient sacred congener and present inhabitant of Egypt.

When we first see them they are generally manipulating the ball — a small mass of manure in which an egg has been laid, and which by rolling in the dust has now become round and firmly incrusted and smooth. Let us follow the couple in their apparently aimless though no less expeditious and vehement labors. They have now brought their globular charge through the grassy stubble, and have reached a clear spot of earth with scattered weeds. Of course we all know from the books that their intention is to find a suitable spot in which to bury this ball, and such being the case, with what astonishing stupidity do they urge on that labor! Here certainly is just the right spot for you, Mrs. Tumble-bug! Stop rolling and dig! But no, she will not listen to reason. She mounts the top of the ball, and, creeping far out upon it, pulls it over forward with her back feet, while Mr. Tumble-bug helps her in a most singular fashion. Does he stand up on his hind legs on the opposite side, and push with his powerful front feet? Oh no; he stands on his head, and pushes with his hind legs. As he pushes, and as the ball rolls merrily on, Mrs. Tumble-bug is continually rolled around with it, and must needs climb backward at a lively rate to keep her place. A foot or two is thus travelled without special incident, when a slight trouble occurs. The ball has struck an obstacle which neither Mrs. Tumble-bug's pull nor Mr. Tumble-bug's push can overcome. Then follow an apparent council and interchange of Tumble-bug. talk, until at length both put their shovel-

shaped heads together beneath the sphere, and over it goes among the weeds. It is soon out again upon the open. Now, Mrs. Tumble-bug, everything is plain-sailing for you; here is a long down grade over the smooth clean dirt! Why, the ball would roll down itself if you would only let it; but, no, she will *not* let it. She pauses, and the ball rests, and both beetles now creep about, shovelling up the dirt here and there with their very queer little flat heads. Ah, perhaps they are going to start that *hole* which all the books tell us about. But no; the place is evidently not quite satisfactory, both of them seem so to conclude, like two souls with but a single thought. Mrs. T. is up on the bridge in a jiffy, and Mr. T. takes his place at the helm; and now what an easy time they will have of it down this little slope; but, no, again; tumble-bugs don't seem to care for an easy time. A hundred times on their travels will they pass the very best possible spot for that burrow, a hundred times will they persist in guiding that little world of theirs over an obstruction, when a clear path lies an inch to the right or left of them. And here, when their labors might be so easily lightened by a downward grade, what do they do? they deliberately turn the ball about and hustle it along *up hill*, and that, too, over dirt that is not half as promising. Tip they go! Mrs. T. now seems to have the best of it, and I sometimes have my suspicions whether she is not playing a prank on that unsuspecting spouse working so hard at her back, for he now has not only the ball, but Mrs. T. as well, to shove along, for the most that she can do is to throw the weight of her body forward, which in a steep up grade amounts to nothing as a help.

But if she is imposing on Mr. T. in thus guiding the ball up hill, she soon gets the Roland for her Oliver. Mr. T. is put to great extra labor by this whimsical decision of hers, and woe to Mrs. T. when that little chance valley or inequality of surface is reached. Even though she can see it coming and holds the wheel, she rarely seems to take advantage of it to save herself or her ship, while Mr. T., going backward in the rear, of course cannot be expected to know what is coming, nor be blamed for the consequences. With kick after kick from his powerful hind feet, united with the push of his mighty pair in front, the ball speeds up the slope. Now, for some reason, he gives a backward shove of more than usual force when it was least necessary. The ball had chanced upon the crest of a slope, when, kick! over it goes with a pitch and a bound, and Mrs. T. with it, though this time not on top. Happy is she if the ball simply rolls upon her and pins her down. Such, indeed, is a frequent episode in her experience of keeping the ball a-rolling, but occasionally the tumble-ball thus started, and out of the control of her spouse at the rear, may roll over and over for a long distance, but never alone. No amount of demoralization of this sort ever surprises her into losing her grip on her precious globular bundle. When at last it fetches up against a stone or stick, and she assures herself that she and her charge are safe and sound, no doubt she immediately mounts to its crest to signal the lone Mr. T. afar off, who is quickly back of her again, and both are promptly off on a fresh journey. And so they keep it up, apparently for sport, perhaps for an hour.

At length, when they have played long enough —for there is no other reason apparent to *homo sapiens*—they decide to plant their big, dirty pellet. The place which they have chosen is not half as promising as many they have passed, but that doesn't seem to matter. Mrs. T. has said, "It shall go here," and that ends it.

Then follows a most singular exhibition of excavation and burial. The ball is now resting quietly on the dirt, and the two beetles are apparently rummaging around beneath it, trying the ground with the sharp edge of their shovel-shaped faces. And now, to avoid confusion, we will dismiss Mr. T., and confine our observation strictly to the female, who usually (in my experience) conducts the rest of the work alone.

She has evidently found a spot that suits her, and we expect her to fulfil the directions of the books and entomological authorities. She must "dig a deep hole first, and then roll the ball into it, and fill it up again." But we will look in vain for such obedience. Instead of this she persists in ploughing around beneath the ball, which seems at times almost balanced on her back, until all the earth at this point is soft and friable, and she is out of sight under it. Presently she appears again at the surface, and as quickly disappears again, this time going in upsidedown beneath the ball, which she pulls downward with her pair of middle feet, while at the same time, with hind legs and powerful digging front legs, she pushes outward and upward the loose earth which she has accumulated. Visibly the ball sinks into the cavity moment by moment as the earth is lowered for a space of half an inch in the surrounding soil, and continually forced upward outside of its circumference. In a few moments the pellet has sunk level with the ground, and in a few moments more the loose earth pushed upward has overtopped it and it is out of sight. Still, for hours this busy excavator continues to dig her hole and pull the ball in after her, with shovel head and mole-like digging feet scooping out a circular well much larger than the diameter of the ball, which slowly sinks by its own weight, aided by her occasional downward pull, as this same loosened earth is pushed upward above it. The burrow is thus sunk several inches, when the beetle ploughs her way to the surface and is ready for another similar experience.

The remaining history of the ball and its change is soon told. The egg within it soon hatches, the larva finding just a sufficiency of food to carry it to its full growth, when it transforms to a chrysalis, and at length to the tumble-bug like its parent. The formerly loose earth above him is now firmly packed, but he seems to know by instinct why those powerful front feet were given

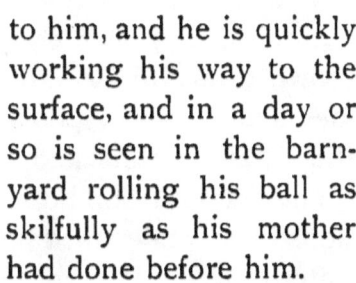

to him, and he is quickly working his way to the surface, and in a day or so is seen in the barnyard rolling his ball as skilfully as his mother had done before him.

Such is the method always employed by the tumble-bug as I have seen him. And yet I have read in many natural histories, and have heard careful observers claim, that the hole is dug first and the ball rolled in. Perhaps they vary their plan, but I doubt it. Here is a matter for some of our boys and girls to look into.

Those Horse-hair Snakes

SO they are called; and if the almost unanimous rustic opinion, with its ancient tradition and reliable witness, is to be credited, such they are in very truth. Indeed, there would seem to be few better attested facts in the whole range of natural history than the pedigree of this white or brown thread-like creature which is found in summer shallows and pools. Go where you will in the rural districts and it is the same old story. "They come from horse-hairs," and in some sections they are destined finally to become full-grown water-adders. It is commonly no mere theory. It is either an indisputable fact, tested by individual observation, or else is accepted as a matter of course, much as Pliny of old accepted the similar natural history "discoveries" of his time. He says, for example, on a similar subject, "I have heard many a man say that the marrow of a man's backbone will breed to a snake. And well it may so be, for surely there be many secrets in nature to us unknown, and much may come of hidden causes."

I have exchanged much comment on the subject of the hair snake with New England farmers. I have heard it claimed by one rural authority that a horse-hair bottled in water and placed in the sun will become a snake at second full moon. One prominent Granger, not to be outdone, went so far as to affirm that an old horse of his fell dead at the edge of the dam, and that the whole animal's tail squirmed off, and the pond was full of hair snakes in consequence. It becomes almost a matter of personal offence to the average countryman to question the truth of these statements. The hair snake is a *fact*—settled by their forefathers, and more true than ever to-day.

But snake stories, like fish stories, are always to be "taken with salt," and lest some of our younger readers may become converts to the rural authorities with whom they are perhaps associated in the summer outings, and in order also to relieve our long-suffering horse from this outrageous libel on its tail, it is well to settle our horse-hair snake story once and for all. To this end, I doubt if I can do better than to quote from memory a certain village store discussion of which the everlasting hair snake was the topic. I say "discussion," but this was hardly the proper term to apply to a general conversation in which all the parties seemed to agree. For some moments it consisted of anecdotes bearing on the subject, and each of the group had furnished his item of interest supporting the accepted theory of the horsehair origin of the snake. Only one member of the company remained to be heard from, Amos Shoopegg, the village cobbler, who had kept silent, with somewhat sinister expression on his countenance as he listened with a sort of superior disdain to the various wonderful accounts, until at length, upon the recital of the story of the dead horse in the pond, he could contain himself no longer, and blurted out:

"Well, I swan, I never see sech a lot of dunceheels! I never hear sech fool talk since I's born. They ain't one on ye thet's got enny sense."

"Waal, haow much hev *yeu* gut?" asked the narrator of the dead-horse story, testily. "*Yeu* never see a har snake in yer life, and wouldn't know one from a side o' sole-leather er a waxed-end ef it wuz laid in yer lap."

"Not know 'em? I guess not," replied Amos. "I know more about 'em than the hull lot o' ye put together. Not know 'em! Law! hain't I seen 'em flyin' over the meddy by the hundreds in hayin'-time!"

A loud and long-continued guffaw concert greeted this surprising statement, a result which the shrewd cobbler had anticipated.

"We give in," remarked one sarcastic snake expert, when the laughter had subsided. "We give in. We don't enny on us know *thet* much," followed by another burst of derisive laughter.

"Thet's becuz yeu ornery critters hain't gut no sense," replied Amos, with warmth. "Ye beleve jest wut ennybody tells ye, or jest wut yer gran'ther beleved before ye, ez though *yeur* gran'ther knowed any more'n a hedge fence jest becuz he hed the misfortoon to be *yeur* gran'ther. *My* gran'ther sed so tew. But what on't? He warn't to blame. He didn't know no better. I *do*. Yeu say them snakes come from hoss-har. Like nuff they ain't one o' ye but b'leeves fer a fac' thet ef yer old har-cloth sofy wuz put to soak it wou'd all squirm off overnight. Ye see these ar har snakes in the hoss-trawf, and thet's *enuff* fer ye. Immejetly yeu hev yer 'hoss-har snake,' 'n' you're so sot they ain't no livin' with ye."

And so he went on, with occasional exclamatory or chaffing interruptions.

"Oh yis! Yeu know all about 'em, jest becuz ye hed a gran'ther who wuz a dunceheels. Nobody kin teech ye nothin', but *I'll* tek a leetle o' the conceit out o' ye afore I'm done with ye. Wut I know I *know*, 'n' wut I say I kin prove. 'N' if none o' yeu idjits hain't seen them har snakes a-flyin' over the meddy ez I sed, then ye *don't know nothin' about 'em.* I tell ye I've seen 'em 'n' caught 'em!"

"Say, Amos," slyly asked a jibing neighbor at his elbow, "wut did ye hev in the hayin'-pail that day?"

"Waal," drawled Amos, after the momentary laughter had subsided, "wutever it wuz, it 'd do yeu a power o' good ef yeu'd take one long pull on't. It would be a eye-opener fer ye, p'r'aps, 'n' yeu'd *larn* suthin'. You've ben fed with a spoon all yer life, 'n' ye swaller wutever they give ye without lookin'. Thet's wut ails *yeu.* Say," he continued, trying to get in a word edgewise in the prevalent hilarious din, "you idjits er havin' a mighty sight o' fun over this 'ere! I'll give ye a chance to show which on ye is the biggest fool. Doos any one o' ye want to bet me that ye ain't a pack o' dunces? Which on ye 'll bet me a scythe that wut I say about these ar flyin' snakes is all poppycut? Come, naow, I'm talkin' bizniss, and if ye ain't a lot o' cowards, p'r'aps you'll *prove* thet ye ain't. I say them snakes wuz a-flyin' around ez fast ez grasshoppers all over the meddy, 'n' ar flyin' thar naow, like all-possessed, 'n' I kin *prove* it. Naow who sez I *kain't,* and will wager me a new scythe on't?"

A momentary lull followed this challenge, but

the bet was promptly taken by several of the company, the "dead-horse" story-teller being the first to rise to the bait.

In a moment Amos had left the store, and within a half-hour (barely long enough for him to have reached his home and returned) he reappeared with a box containing the "proofs" of his remarkable statement.

He won his bet, having introduced his sceptical hearers to the two prime authorities that knew more about hair snakes than all the rustic wiseacres or scientific professors put together, for his box was filled with grasshoppers and black crickets, including one or two specimens specially preserved in a small vial of alcohol, to show the parasitic snake coiled in its close spiral.

It is reported that Amos never got his scythe, however, the "dead-horse" story-teller having backed out on a technicality, claiming that Amos could not have seen the snakes, he said, and that the snakes had no wings, and consequently could not have been seen "flying" over the meadow; but the cobbler was at least the means of wiping out the hair-snake superstition in the village, and even to this day he is heard to sing out to the chaffing group at the village store, on occasions when he is crowded a little too far, "Who sed hoss-har snake?" He laughs best who laughs last.

There was nothing in the outward appearance of Amos to indicate an intelligence superior to that of his fellows, the secret of his present victorious position being found in the fact that he had been in the habit of making the most of his "summer boarders." One of these, during the present season, had been a college professor of biology, who had enlightened him on many puzzling matters of natural history, including the mystery of the hair snake, whose horse-hair origin he would once have maintained as stoutly as did his opponents at the village store.

My own early belief was influenced by the prevailing country opinion, and more than one is the horse hair which I have put to soak with interesting anticipation. By a mere accident the true source of the snake was discovered. I had procured a box of grasshoppers and crickets for bait, numbering some hundreds, and once, upon opening it, observed two of the thread-like creatures entangled like a snell among the insects. Further experience while baiting the hooks with the grasshoppers revealed others in the bodies of both crickets and grasshoppers, which seemed in no way disturbed by their presence.

So the "horse-hair snake" may be written down a myth. Its existence prior to the time we discover it in the brook or puddle has been spent under the hospitable roof of the insects mentioned, upon escaping from which it seeks the water to lay its eggs. The young in turn seek the grasshoppers and crickets which frequent their haunt, and thus the routine is continued, to the possible annoyance of the grasshopper and the complete mystification of the rural scientist.

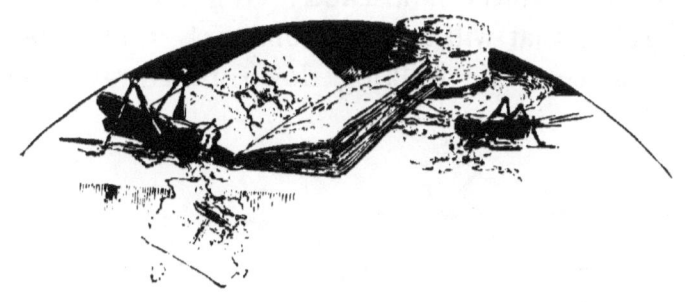

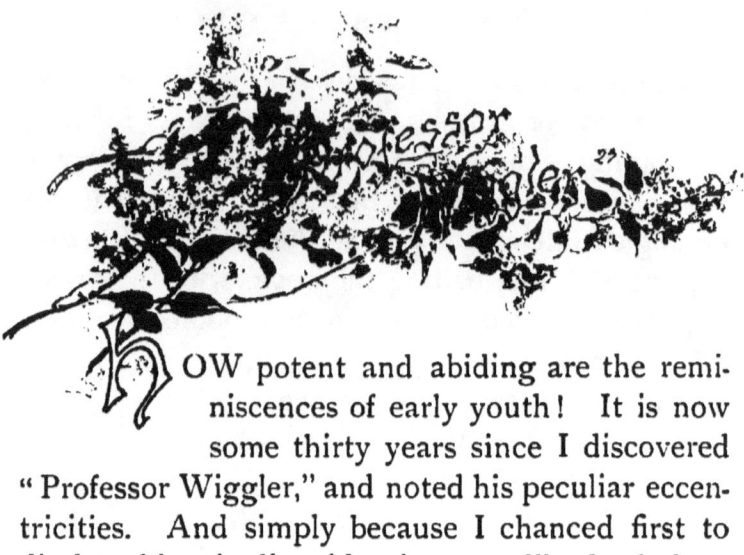

Professor Wiggler

HOW potent and abiding are the reminiscences of early youth! It is now some thirty years since I discovered "Professor Wiggler," and noted his peculiar eccentricities. And simply because I chanced first to disclose his wiggling identity on a lilac-bush, how irresistibly must his comical presence assert itself with my slightest thought of lilac, with the shape of its leaf, the faintest whiff of its fragrance, or even a distant glimpse of its spray!

Yonder, for instance, an old ruin of a home closely hemmed in with the well-known bushes spots the wintry landscape. What a place for Wigglers that will be next summer! Only a few days since, while walking down Broadway, New

York, I paused for a momentary glimpse of a fine display of spring silks in a shop window, when Professor Wiggler, without the slightest rhyme or reason, suddenly wagged his comical head across my fancy, for my thoughts were far from professors and entomology. Following a frequent, quiet pastime of mine, of tracing the pedigree of such vagrant waifs of thought, I fell to pondering what could have summoned my unbidden friend, and I soon discovered. Why, how simple! The window before me was a very epitome of tender vernal hues—blushes of pale blossoms, yellows of pale anthers shadowed under petals, and quickened grays of bourgeoning hill-side woods, warm pulsing greens of budding leaves, each fabric bearing its label of the latest color-fad—coral gray, Chinese pink, primrose ash, old rose, and yonder was a faded purple bearing the title "lilac," which, of course, by its own irresistible telegraph through my retina, had called up the professor, and here he was.

Yes, it must be admitted, he is a rather unceremonious and promiscuous professor, but I can nevertheless recommend him to our young people as a most amusing and entertaining character. As I have said, I first made his acquaintance over thirty years ago, and in spite of his obtrusive ways in season and out of season, I nevertheless renew our actual acquaintance on the lilac-bush every summer, and I am always greeted with the same expressive "wiggle-waggle."

It was in early August when I first discovered

him, a small brown and white crook-backed creature about an inch long, clothed with scattered hairs, and clinging to the edge of a leaf, half of which he had eaten to the mid rib. As I approached he ceased eating, and began to wag his upraised head and body vehemently, and I promptly named him Wiggler, subsequently adding the "professor" for special reasons which I do not now recall. Careful search about the bush led to the discovery of a dozen or more of the caterpillars, all about the same size; and such was their novelty among the young insect-collectors that wigglers now became all the rage, and were at a premium on trade. The lilac-bushes of the town were scoured for caterpillars, and there was suddenly a "corner" on wigglers. A Professor Wiggler was now worth two bull's-eyes, and even two classical Polyphemuses, or three *Attacus prometheus* cocoons were considered only a just and dignified equivalent for a full-grown specimen of the new professor. For those which I had first found proved to be mere infants. As they waxed fat and healthy and lively on their daily supply of fresh lilac leaves, they soon reached the length of quite an inch and a half, and their humps and zigzag outline were proportionately

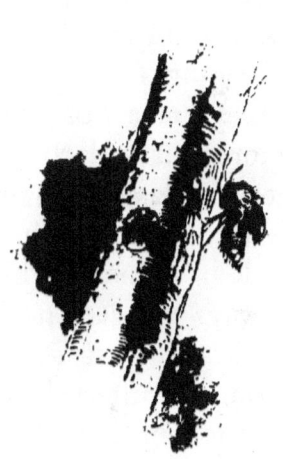

developed, to say nothing of their wiggling propensities.

How well I remember the "whack! whack! whack!" from the inside of the pasteboard or wooden box as I entered the room, or chanced to make the slightest commotion in its neighborhood, as the captive pets threatened to dash their brains out in their demonstrations at my approach. Opening the box, I was always greeted with the same concert of whisking heads, the action being more particularly expressive from the long projecting lash of hairs, an inch and a quarter in length, with which the caterpillar's head was provided. One singular feature of these hairs had always puzzled me in the earlier life of the caterpillar, but was soon explained by close observation. At intervals of every quarter of an inch or so in the length of the slender tuft we find, in perfect specimens, a tiny brown speck—perhaps three or four—graduating in size to the tip of the hairs, where the atom is scarcely visible, or generally absent. A careful examination of their shape revealed the fact that they were exactly like the heads of the younger caterpillars in all their stages, and their presence and successive accumulation were readily explained by the moulting habits of the caterpillar, which is common to all caterpillars. By these telltale tokens we know that the professor has changed his clothes

—let us see, one, two, three, four—perhaps five times.

When he first emerged from the egg on the lilac-leaf he was indeed a tiny atom; his head would make a small show laid upon our page. When about a week old, by dint of a good appetite and voracious feeding, he had managed to "outgrow his skin," as it were. He could literally hold no more, and realizing that nature would come to his relief, he began to spin a tiny web upon the leaf-stalk in which to secure his hooked feet for a temporary rest, sleeping off his dinner, as it were.

He is now a very quiet and circumspect young professor. It were indeed a dangerous experiment to wiggle in such a tight suit as now incloses him, so he remains immovable and resigned. A strange process is now going on in his physiology. Hour by hour his outer skin is becoming detached from the under skin, and now he is simply inclosed within its sac. The shell of his former head has been crowded off his face, as it were, and has slid down towards the mouth of the new head within. Shortly after this feature has taken place the imprisoned caterpillar becomes restless to burst his bonds, and a quiet working motion begins, which gradually forces the skin in wrinkles towards the tail of the body, of course drawing it tighter and tighter about the head, and with it the connection from the spiracles at the sides of the body. At last, with one final effort, the skin behind the head ruptures, and discloses the new skin beneath, and through the opening thus made the new head soon appears, and the entire new suit of clothes emerges in a few moments. But though the old clothes are worked off into a little shrunken pellet at the tail, the old head-shell is still retained, being attached to the hairs immediately back of the new head, and thus retained. Five or six times in the life of the caterpillar this same process is performed, each performance leaving its token; so that our "professor" enjoys the unique distinction of being able, in his mature years, to look up to the head he wore when he was a baby or youngster, and make it useful, too, in keeping off the flies as he ponders on the flight of time.

But this is not all our professor's peculiarities. One day, as I came to look at my hump-backed pets, I discovered that most of them had shrunk a full third, and had refused to eat and, what surprised me more, refused to wiggle. A closer examination of the box showed that while they had ignored the lilac leaves, they had been gnawing the pasteboard everywhere in the box, even perforating it with a number of holes. The captives in a thin wooden box were similarly affected, and numbers of holes were to be seen. What did it mean? I had been expecting daily to see my full-grown caterpillars either beginning their cocoons or suspending themselves by their tails in readiness for the chrysalis state. Yet they had done neither. Their time had evidently come, but they were not satisfied with their surroundings, and would seem to wish to escape; and yet, having gnawed their way to liberty, deliberately remained in prison! It was some days before I correctly interpreted their curious contradictory actions, and as I remember it now, my hint came from a spider-web which had spread its catch all beneath a lilac-bush, and upon which I discerned a number of tiny balls of sawdust which had chanced to fall upon it. Looking directly above, among the branches, I soon found a wiggler, not only gnawing the wood but with one-third of its body in a burrow in a twig the size of my finger. I had observed him thus for a few moments when he began to back out, drawing with him a tiny ball of sawdust, which he threw out with a slight wiggle, and soon resumed operations.

Leaving him to his work, I lost no time in taking the hint, and my box was soon criss-crossed with small twigs, and my remaining wigglers soon found themselves at home and littered my box with their chip pellets. The burrow is first made diagonally to the pith, and then follows the centre for about two-thirds of an inch. I remember hav-

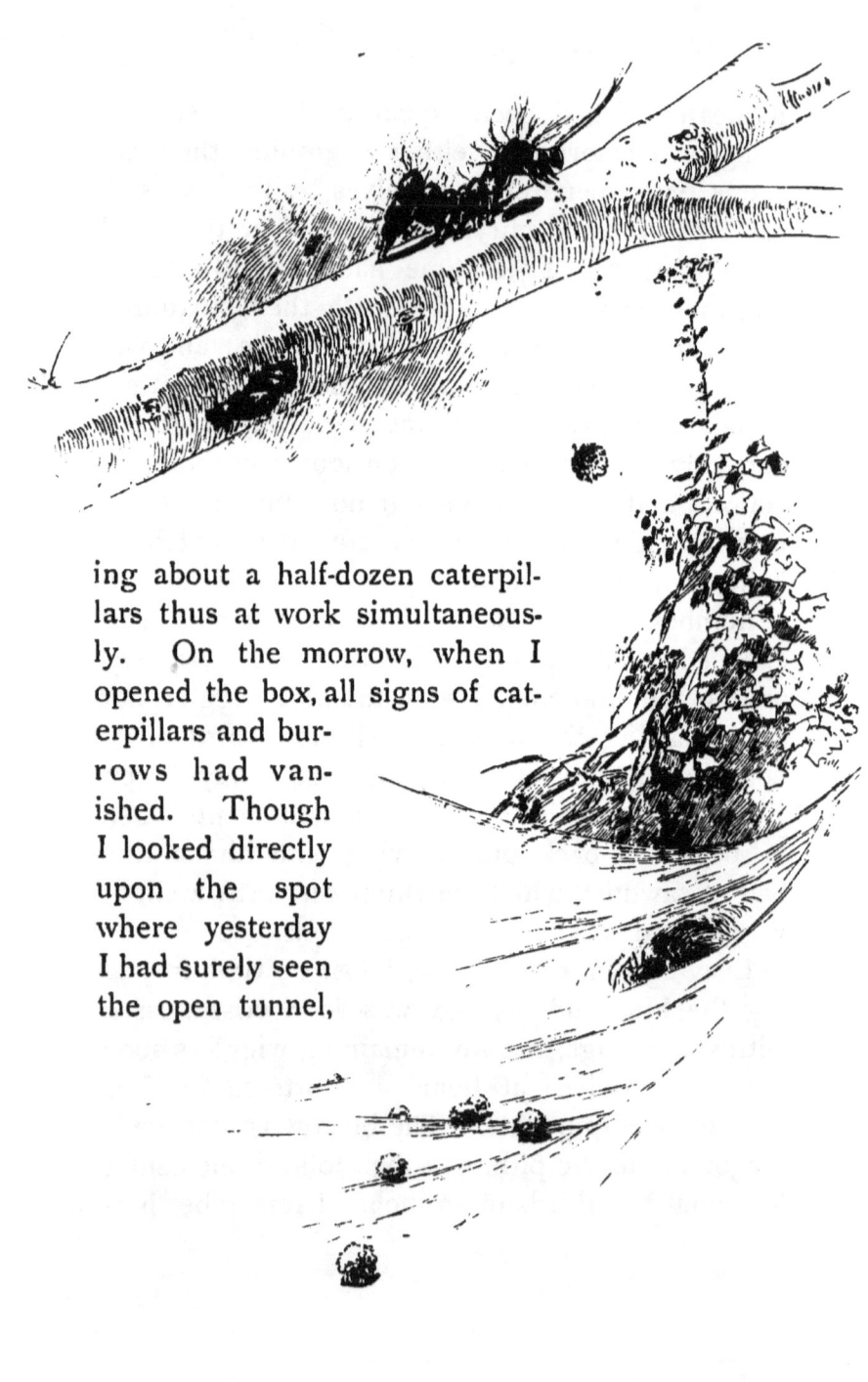

ing about a half-dozen caterpillars thus at work simultaneously. On the morrow, when I opened the box, all signs of caterpillars and burrows had vanished. Though I looked directly upon the spot where yesterday I had surely seen the open tunnel, no vestige of it now appeared, and its whereabouts could only be guessed by the slight rose-colored stain which the caterpillar had left on the bark below. What had happened?

The burrows had been completed in the night, and the caterpillars had retired into them, backward presumably, and then spun over the opening by a disk of silk, which they had finally, or in the process, tinted the exact color of the external surrounding bark. I have frequently exhibited one of these sticks, with its inclosed caterpillar, to curious friends, who were unable to locate, without long and careful scrutiny, the mysterious curtain. The twig, dried in a mild oven so as to kill the inclosed caterpillar, or with its farther side split off for his removal, would serve as an interesting permanent specimen, the delicate disk being otherwise ruptured by the final escape of the moth.

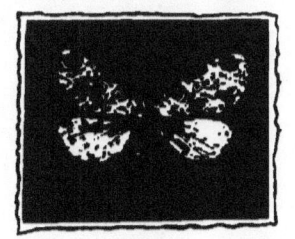

All of mine appeared in the first week of July of the next year. They were small, for the size of the caterpillar, yellowish-white "millers," the fore wings beautifully mottled and banded with brown, and each with three conspicuous round spots of dull red, which feature has secured the insect its specific name of "Trisignata"—*Gramatophora trisignata* being the name of our professor in learned circles.

His burrowing habits do not seem to be generally known, the only mention of which I have chanced to observe merely alluding to the fact that the "caterpillar has the unusual power of boring very smooth cylindrical holes in solid pine wood." But Professor Wiggler does not bore wood for a pastime, as we have seen.

"Cow-spit, Snake-spit and Frog-spit"

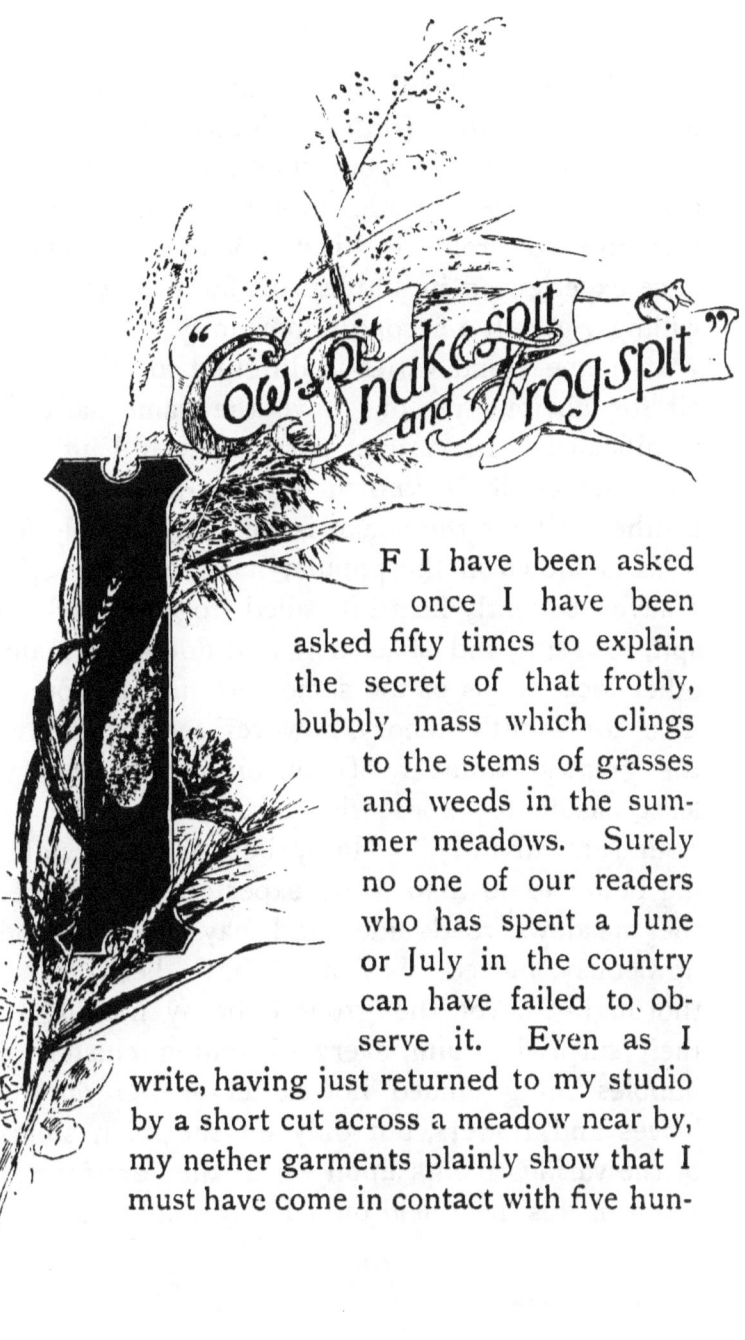

IF I have been asked once I have been asked fifty times to explain the secret of that frothy, bubbly mass which clings to the stems of grasses and weeds in the summer meadows. Surely no one of our readers who has spent a June or July in the country can have failed to observe it. Even as I write, having just returned to my studio by a short cut across a meadow near by, my nether garments plainly show that I must have come in contact with five hundred of them during these few rods. In the height of its season this frothy nuisance monopolizes many a meadow. No one, unless most ordinarily clad, would care to wade through its slimy haunt. Certainly no stroller in his "Sunday best," having once experienced its unpleasant familiarity, would willingly give it a second opportunity.

Its name, I find, varies in different localities, but all, for obvious reasons, have the same salivary significance. In various parts of New England, for instance, it is known as cow-spit. In the southern States the snake is held responsible for it, as is shown in the popular name of snake-spit. I have frequently heard it called frog-spit, cuckoo-spit, toad-spit, and sheep-spit, and doubtless many other local terms of the same sort may be found. The cow-spittle theory, however, seems to have the greatest number of converts. Let me, at least, hasten to expose this miserable slander on "our rural divinity." Have, then, our cows nothing better to do than to go expectorating all over the meadows, road-sides, and hay-fields? And how busy, indeed, they must have been to so thoroughly cover the ground, to say nothing of their surprising aim, every glistening cluster of bubbles being landed not helter-skelter on the leaves and flowers, but only on the main stems of the various plants upon which they are found! Even in this little field outside my studio window, which is thus generously moistened, what a task! Why, it would certainly have taken at least ten cows in industrious expectoration to have left it so profusely decorated as now; but the fact is, there is not, nor has there been, a single cow in the field.

Only a few weeks ago I received a letter from an Ohio boy who, among other things, wanted to know what those slimy "gobs" on alders came from. He said they called them "snake-spit" out there, but that he had seen lots of them higher than any snake could get, unless it was a "racer," meaning the blacksnake, which, as is well known, is fond of climbing trees and bushes. And later came a letter from a lady in Lewiston, North Carolina, who had looked deeper into the matter, and whose inquiry throws a little light on the subject. She writes as follows:

"An old subscriber to 'Harper's Young People' desires to express the pleasure which your articles have afforded.... I have just finished the last, and have been out to examine the faded primroses, but only a long-legged green spider rewarded my search. Too late for our season." The readers of "Young People" will recall my article about the beautiful rosy moth which lives in the faded evening primrose, and which was the quest of the above writer, who further continues: "I do not think you have written about what is called here 'snake's-spittle,' a frothy exudation, perfectly white, surrounding a small speckled beetle (I suppose). I found several on my chrysanthemums about two weeks ago, but they seem to have disappeared now."

This supposed "small speckled beetle" lets out the secret of our "cow-spittle." The old cow is acquitted, and also the snake, who has enough mischief to answer for.

Each of these masses of bubbles is seen to surround the stem, upon which it clings, out of consideration to the popular tradition, spitted through the centre, as it were, with its culm of grass or branch of bramble or weed. But the true expectorator is within, laved in his own froth, his beak embedded in the juicy stem, and his suds factory continually at work. We have only to blow or scrape off the white bubbles, and we shall disclose him, even though he makes considerable effort to dodge out of sight, either in the remnant froth or around the stem. But it is not a beetle that we at last bring to view. It would be hard, indeed, for any one but a naturalist to decide on so short an acquaintance precisely what to call him. He is green and speckled in color, anywhere from a quarter to half an inch in length, depending upon his age, and somewhat to be anticipated in the extent of his show of suds. He is wide of brow, has rather prominent eyes, and tapers off somewhat wedge-shaped behind.

To the bug student these features are very significant, and he is not long in placing the creature among his proper kindred. He has a sucking beak, which connects him with the tribe of bugs, and other features ally him to the cicada, a humble though accomplished relative of the buzzing harvest-fly or hornet. He dwells in cool contentment here in his aerated bath, but he has not thus put himself to soak as the end and aim of his existence. Erelong he will graduate from these moist surroundings, and we shall see quite another sort of being, whom we would not dare to affront by the mere mention of such an ignominious, foamy existence. Here is one of them, which has just flown in around our evening lamp, and has settled upon my paper as I write. Not a strange coincidence, by any means, for others very like him have been there before when I have been writing on various other topics, and are the certain representatives of that nocturnal swarm which is always attracted by the light.

What a pretty atom he is as he rests here on my paper, clad in his bright emerald green, and only about a quarter of an inch in length! Let us catch him for our cabinet. But this is not so simple, for, like the proverbial flea, I put my finger on him, and he isn't there, but is to be seen yonder, at the farther edge of the table, the instant I lift my finger-tip. And there are others like him scattered about me beneath the lamp, one especially with four brilliant scarlet bands on his bright green wings, a near relative, though I am not sure at this moment whether he dates back to such a soaking as his little emerald fellow just described. We must be quick indeed to catch him, he is so alert; and while his entire visible emerald anatomy consists of a pair of nimble wings, no one would guess it now, for he certainly does not use them as he speeds here and there on our table. No, he has still another resource in those powerful hind legs of his, which soon take him out of our reach when he concludes to trust the spring. Here, then, is one of the host of midgets who are responsible for our soiled garments in our summer walks—the "frog-hopper," or "spume-bearer," in his perfection. The round of his life is thus given in Harris's beautiful volume, " Insects Injurious to Vegetation ":

" The 'frog-hoppers' pass their whole lives on plants, on the stems of which their eggs are laid in the autumn. The following summer they are hatched, and the young immediately perforate the bark with their beaks, and begin to imbibe the sap. They take in such quantities of this that it oozes out of their bodies continually in the form of little bubbles, which soon completely cover up the insects. They thus remain entirely buried and concealed in large masses of foam until they have completed the final transformation, on which account the names of cuckoo-spittle, frog-spittle, and frog-hopper have been applied to them. The spittle in which they are sheltered may be seen in great abundance during the summer on the stems of our alders and willows. In the perfect state they are not thus protected, but are found on the plants in the latter part of summer fully grown, and preparing to lay their eggs. In this state they possess the power of leaping in a remarkable degree, and for this purpose the tips of their hind shanks are surrounded with little spines."

The "spume-bearer" (*Aphrophora*) this insect

has been called, and the peculiar method by which he turns out the froth on the stem is well worth a little study. He makes no secret of the process. If we take a grass stem, remove him from his liquid lair, and transfer him to another stem, we may witness a novel method in the preparation of suds. And a busy little factory it is, too, when we consider what a continuous demand is made upon it, caused by the sun's evaporation through the long summer day. A single mass of bubbles with its tenant removed quickly disappears. If the little insect is permitted to crawl upon our hand, he is apt to try the new domicile. I have never been able to induce him to continue up to the suds point, but have no trouble in locating the place where he begins operations.

Wasp He Doings

FEW of our common insects enjoy a wider intimate acquaintance with or a more respectful recognition from humanity than the wasps and hornets. Their acquaintance, with that of their yellow-jacket bee and bumble-bee relatives, is forced upon most of us at a tender and impressionable age, and leaves a lasting reminiscence. Having once been interviewed by a hornet, do we not remember him for life for his pains?

The bee has perhaps given us equally pointed excuse for respectful, or rather disrespectful, consideration, and yet how different is our attitude to the bee in contrast with that towards the hornet! Why? The discrimination is largely a matter of sentiment, but especially a matter of ignorance; sentiment as associated with fragrant flowers and droning wings and "white-clover honey"—for do we not all know the "busy bee," and how he "gathers honey all the day" for the hive, and thus for humanity and the hot biscuit? There is then a palliative for the busy bee's "hot foot," as Paddy described his first warm contact with the insect. But who ever heard of any one with a good word for the hornet? He is under the ban—an outlaw, the black sheep of the insect fraternity, a source of uneasy suspicion, shunned by valiant man, good for nothing to the boy except to shy stones at from a safe retreat; while to the fair sex, always the signal for precipitate flight, if not hysterical terror.

The popular verdict on the hornet is so well voiced in that famous entomological essay from the pen of Josh Billings that I am tempted to quote it entire and use it for my present text. I am sure the average reader will say "Amen" to every word of it:

"The hornet is a red-hot child ov Nature ov sudden impreshuns and a sharp konklusion. The hornets alwus fites at short range and never argy a case. They settle all ov their disputes bi letting their javelin fly, an' are az certain an' az anxious tew hit az a mule iz. Hornets bild their nest wherever they take a noshun to, an' seldum are asked to move; for what good is it tew murder 99 hornets an' have the one hundred one hit you with his javelin! I kan't tell you just tew a day how long a hornet kan live, but I kno from experience that every bug, be he hornet or somebody else who is mad all the time, an' stings every chance he kan git, generally outlives all ov his nabors."

An artistically constructed paragraph, with a "snapper" at the end of it, or rather a "sharp konklusion" quite consistent with its subject.

"Mad all the time," he says, and "stings every chance he can git," and such would seem to be the unanimous belief. Indeed, the phrase "As mad as a hornet" has passed into a proverb, which presumably dates back to the Aryans, or at least from the scriptural allusion of the providential visitation of hornets, which routed the impious inhabitants of Canaan before the conquering Israelites. The ancient Greeks and Latins are on record in their appreciation of the "warlike hornet," and considered that it came rightly by its valor as an inheritance from the dead war-horse from whose carcass the insects were supposed to be spontaneously generated.

"The warlike horse if buried underground
Shortly a brood of hornets will be found,"

writes Ovid. Another author, Cardanus, thought

that a dead mule was the more likely source, which recalls the above erudite allusion of hereditary instinct of Billings.

Yes, if time-honored popular prejudice is to be accepted, the hornet is always on the rampage, always spoiling for a fight, always "mad"; and considering how many thousands of them there are abroad, and what opportunity they have of mischief, it is a wonder that poor humanity is able to put its nose out of doors with impunity.

Let us see how far this bad reputation is sustained by the facts. What is this black paper hornet (more properly wasp) doing from morning till night? Buzzing among the flowers, creeping over the bruised apple windfalls in the orchard, whirling and dodging about the window or fence or side of the house, or perhaps darting in our faces as we sit at the open window.

Two episodes which I recall, in which this white-tailed black wasp from the big paper nest was conspicuous, occur to me as I write, and as the two stories, taken together, will show us the true character of the suspect, and what he is up to all day long, I will narrate them.

The first instance is vivid in my memory. It occurred in my boyhood — *my* boyhood? how many another boy remembers the same incident. That same hot day in August, that same cool,

shadowy swimming-hole in the brook, that same gray paper nest on the overhanging branch a few rods up stream? What a tempting target! How the stones flew as, safe up to our necks in water, if need be, we pelted the paper domicile! And now a lucky throw has gone straight to the mark. With a crushing thud the stone has penetrated the side and knocked off a piece of the gray wall, which falls to the stream below, exposing the tiers of paper comb, as a whirling, buzzy maze, like a swarm of bees, enshrouds the mangled house. Ah, what fun! How we laughed at the sport!— for at least ten seconds. Then the tide turned, and how gladly had we possessed the art of the bull-frog, and buried ourselves in the mud until the storm blew over, for the "mad" warlike hornets were upon us. The red-hot child of Nature "was now at short range," and "stinging every chance they could get." "When you see a head hit it," seemed to be the plan of campaign, and of course the heads had to come up once in a while, and erelong were considerably enlarged, principally through inoculation, but let us hope with wisdom as well.

"A mad hornet, and only at a little boyish fun! Look on this picture, and now on this."

I have shown our hornet under exceptional circumstances, when anger may be a positive virtue and a means of grace. Following are some of the every-day capers, which have not helped his reputation, as I observed them on the crowded porch of a summer hotel in the White Mountains several years ago. It was in September, and about twenty guests, mostly ladies and "summer girls," were assembled in a quiet social convention.

Suddenly there was a scream, as one of the fair ones, with a frantic, vigorous stroke of uplifted fan, distorted face, and a cross-eyed glare, clutched her roll of fancy-work and fled to the house. "Did he sting you?" asked her friend, who readily followed her in the door. "The horrid hornet!" she exclaimed. "No, he didn't sting me, but he would have done if I hadn't hit him just that minute. He flew right at me in the *ugliest* way!" The words were hardly out of her mouth when another scream was heard, followed by a general clearing of the piazza. There were now two or three "mad" hornets making themselves generally promiscuous among the guests. At the last general alarm one gentleman, an old bachelor, who sat tilted back in his chair near by, remarked, with an expression of superior disdain at such a silly exhibition of feminine weakness: "Why, ladies, the hornet won't sting you if you'll only let him alone; he has been buzzing around here for an hour, and hasn't stung anybody yet."

At this moment, as fate would have it, the roving hornet chanced to buzz around the speaker, and with a distinct object and deliberate aim plumped itself against his nose, amid a roar of laughter from the gentlemen present, and the complete discomfiture of the victim, who lost his balance and toppled over sideways upon the floor. He was now glad to follow the ladies indoors, and enjoy the fun at his expense. "Well, it might have been expected," he remarked, "after the way you have all been screaming and banging at him. You have got him mad at last, and the innocent spectator has had to suffer in consequence."

I chanced to be sitting within a few feet of the surprised bachelor, and had observed the incident. Indeed, the hornet had once or twice struck me forcibly upon my coat sleeve and shoulder. Concluding that the incident suggested an opportunity for a little pedagogic enlightenment, illustrated by an object-lesson too good to be entirely lost, I sauntered into the hotel parlor, and did what I could to relieve the hornet from the unjust aspersion on his character.

"Did he sting you?" I asked.

"No, he didn't," replied the victim, who, like the ladies whom he had ridiculed, was more surprised than harmed; "but he tried to, and I concluded not to give him a second chance. He struck me so hard that if his sting *had*

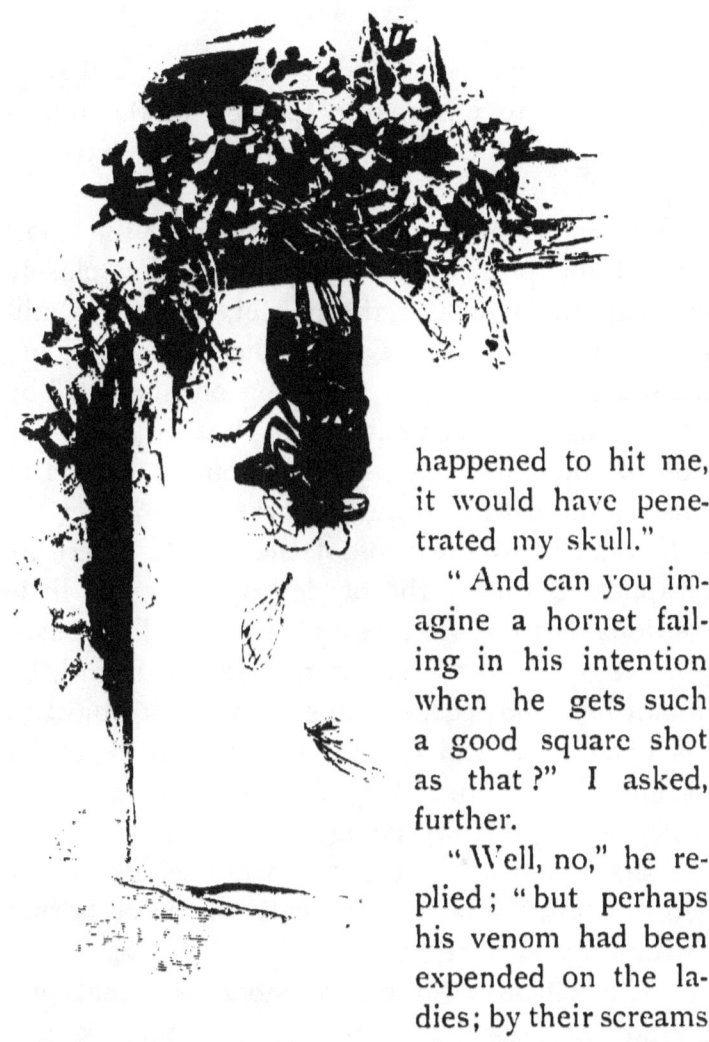

happened to hit me, it would have penetrated my skull."

"And can you imagine a hornet failing in his intention when he gets such a good square shot as that?" I asked, further.

"Well, no," he replied; "but perhaps his venom had been expended on the ladies; by their screams I judge most of them must have been stung a half-dozen times apiece."

"If you will step out on the porch a few moments," I proposed, "I am assured you will soon be disposed to offer your apology to the industrious and innocent insect which you have so libelled."

A cautious group soon assembled at the doorway of the piazza, and at my suggestion closely watched the antics of the hornet, which was still apparently as mad as ever, in the absence of human targets, seemingly "working off his mad" by butting his head against the clapboards along the side of the building. After a moment or two of this exercise, with a quick curvet, the insect betook himself to the roof of the piazza, where he disappeared among the bordering vines. A little cautious search soon revealed his hiding-place, however. He was hanging, head downward, by one of his hind legs, twirling some dark object in his front feet; and it needed only a little closer examination to disclose this object to be a fly, which was gradually being reduced to a pulp by the sharp jaws of its captor—a morsel, doubtless, soon to find its way to the cell of a baby hornet in some paper nest close by.

"You will now doubtless understand that precipitate onslaught on your nose," I remarked to my bachelor friend. "Rest assured that the attraction of that aquiline member alone would never have caused the panic that ensued; but you did not give our hornet the credit for the removal of that pesky fly which had been annoying you for so long, and which is even now being masticated into an unctuous pellet in some secluded corner of the piazza, or is perhaps being borne on buzzing maternal wings to the little white grub in the hornet nest yonder in the pines."

And this is all there is to the "mad" of the hornet. He is generally not half as mad as are his detractors. He is simply minding his own business, and is as busy as a bee in his own way; and if his critics will only mind theirs, there need be no fear that he will try "konklusions" with them, or even give a hint of his "javelin."

This curious episode may be witnessed by any one who will take the trouble to closely observe the wasp. The sunny side of the barn or stable is generally the favorite hunting-ground, and any one who will spend a half-hour in following the efforts of a single wasp will have to admit that he earns his living, for it is not every fly that is caught napping, and that white face, with its eager, open jaws, must needs butt itself against the shingle many times before its quest is satisfied.

But the warlike hornet does not always content himself with such small game as a house-fly. Big bluebottle-flies are a frequent prey, and juicy caterpillars are a welcome variety in his daily diet. Even the butterfly, with a body nearly as large as his own, falls a frequent victim, the scimitar-like jaws severing the painted wings in a twinkling, either during flight, or falling one by one from its dangling retreat.

The life of the black hornet, or wasp, may be briefly summed up. The females survive the winter, and in spring build a tiny comb of papery material composed of saliva and timber scraped from old gray boards and fence rails. In each cell of the comb an egg is laid, which soon hatches into a minute white grub, the sides of the cells being continued to accommodate its growth, the comb being gradually inclosed in the paper covering and enlarged as the nest cells are increased. The grub at maturity incases itself within its cell by closing the orifice with a silken veil, and soon turns to a chrysalis, and in a few days emerges as a perfect wasp. Several broods are reared in a season, the combs being extended in several layers, each suspended by a single stalk from the centre of the one immediately above. A single nest sometimes presents as many as six or seven tiers. But the nests are much more safely examined in winter than in summer.

The Spider's Span

BSERVERS who witnessed from day to day the construction of the great Brooklyn Bridge were often heard to remark, as they looked up with awe from the ferry-boats beneath at the workmen suspended everywhere among the net-work of cables, "Those men look just like spiders in a web." The comparison seemed irresistible, and the writer heard it expressed many times. But how few who gave utterance to the sentiment realized the full significance of the "spider" allusion, or for a moment reflected that the span itself was, in many particulars of its construction, but a parallel of an engineering feat of which the spider was the earliest discoverer. Yet among all the distinguished names engraved upon the memorial

tablet upon the stone bridge-tower the spider gets no credit.

Day after day and week after week we might have seen, travelling back and forth against the sky, a wheel-shaped messenger reeling off its tiny wire. Night and day it was busy, each trip adding one more strand to the growing cable which was to support the great substructure below. And what was this travelling wheel called? "The carrier," or "traveller," if I remember rightly. Why this obviously intentional slight and discourtesy when every field and wood and copse in the country—indeed, on the globe—showed its living example, and bore its myriadfold witness that the "spider" was the only legitimate and proper designation?

In the other most notable suspension-bridge, at Niagara, the time-honored methods of the spider were further and conspicuously recognized, but here again without any courteous engraven acknowledgment on the tablet of fame, so far as I have learned.

A kite was flown from the American shore, and reeled out so as to fall upon the Canadian side, and this initial strand was drawn across, and subsequently strengthened by the travelling reel.

The ends of the added wires were firmly secured at their anchorage, and the completed cable at length re-enforced by guy-ropes.

What is the method of our spider? Ages before the advent of the human engineer he followed the same tactics which we now see him performing in every meadow, or even at our window-sill, or on the bouquet upon our table, linking flower with flower, window-sill with garden fence, bush with bush, tree with tree, with his glistening suspension-bridge spanning the stream, river, and meadow. This wiry thread that tightens across our face as we ride in our carriage, and leaves its tingling "snap" upon our nose, what is this but the model suspension cable of Arachne strengthened a hundredfold by the spider which has travelled back and forth over its course for hours perhaps, each trip leaving a fresh strand, one extremity being anchored on yonder oak in the meadow and the other on the church steeple? Such a cable twenty feet in length is a common challenge in our walks in the open wood road, even making a perceptible motion among the leaves and bending twigs on either side ere it yields to our advance. And to the walker who cares to investigate, a silken bridge a hundred feet in length is not a very exceptional find.

This bridge-building is not confined to any particular month or season, nor to any one species of spider. The autumn will afford us the best opportunity for observation. At that season the spider-egg tufts are turning out their baby spiders by the millions, each a perfect grown spider in miniature, and apparently as skilled at birth in the peculiar arts of its kind as its parents were in their ripe old age. Here is a troop of them upon this drooping branch of wild grape by the river brink. Its leaves are glistening in the loose, rambling tangle which marks their wanderings. They are evidently not satisfied with their present surroundings, and would seem desirous of getting as far as possible from

the neighborhood of their cradle and swaddling-clothes. They are the most independent and self-reliant babies on record. They ask advice from no one — indeed their mother died a year ago, perhaps — but each determines to leave his brothers and sisters, to "see the world" for himself, and paddle his own canoe.

Fancy a first trial trip on a tight-rope from the torch of the Statue of Liberty to Governor's Island! Yet such is the corresponding feat accomplished by this self-reliant acrobat, which a few days or perhaps hours ago was but an egg!

Here is one family of spiderlings upon the grape-vine spray, for instance. They are hanging several yards above the water, and with an ocean, as it were, between them and the distant country upon which their hearts are set. But there is no hesitation or misgiving. Let us closely observe this eager youngster far out upon the point of the leaf. The breeze is blowing across the brook. In an instant, upon reaching the edge of the leaf, the spiderling has thrown up the tip of its body, and a tiny, glistening stream is seen to pour out from its group of spinnerets. Farther and farther it floats, waving across the water like a pennant. Two, three, five, ten, fifteen feet are now seen glistening in the sun. Now it floats in among the herbage upon the opposite bank, and seems reach-

ing out for a foothold. In
a minute more its tip has
brushed against a tall group
of asters, and clings fast, the

loose span sagging in the
breeze, and as we turn our
attention to the spider,

we see that he has turned about,
and is now " hauling in the slack,"
which he continues to do until the
span is taut, when he anchors it
firmly to the leaf, and without a

moment's ceremony steps out upon his tight-rope, and makes the "trial trip" across the abyss — a feat which Dr. McCook, the spider specialist and historian, has most felicitously compared to the similar trial trip of Engineer Farrington across the cable of the East River Bridge, a thrilling event which was witnessed by thousands of spectators from sailing craft and housetops.

Our spider has now reached the asters twenty feet away, and is doubtless busying himself by further securing the anchorage at this terminus. It is quickly done, for see, he is even now far out over the water on his return trip, arriving at the grape leaf a moment later. His strand is now three times as strong as at first, and will be many times stronger before he is satisfied with it. An hour later, if we care to go up-stream half a mile to the bridge, or half a mile below to the crossing pole, for the sake of examining those asters across the brook, we shall find our spiderling nicely settled in a tiny little home of his own. The glistening span is now like a tough silken thread, and is moored to the head of flowers by a half-dozen guy-threads in all directions, while in their midst, in the "nave of his tiny wheel of lace," our smart young baby rests from his labors.

Such is the probable course which he would follow, unless, perhaps, his roving spirit, thus tempted, has further asserted itself, and not content with this exploit, he has concluded to span the clouds, and is even now sailing a thousand feet aloft in his " balloon."

As a bridge-builder he has had many successful imitators, but as a balloonist he is yet more than a match for his bigger copyist, *homo sapiens*, as I shall explain in a subsequent paper.

BALLOONING SPIDERS

HE country boy, or I might say even country baby, who does not know a spider-web when he sees it would be considered a curiosity nowadays. The morning gossamer spread in the grass or hung among the weeds and glistening in the dew—who has not seen it, and thought of the agile, long-legged proprietor somewhere lurking near by? And yet for ages, and until a comparatively recent date, this cobweb, either trailing lightly in the breeze or spread in the grass, was a mystery as to its source, and was believed to consist of dew burned by the sun. But the spider has hoodwinked even the wise heads in many other ways, and even to-day is an unsolved mystery to many of us. Yes, we all know the spider-web and the spider, but have we tried to solve the puzzle which he spreads before us by every path, in our window-blind, our office, our bedroom, or even, it may be, in mid-ocean. Here, for instance, a puzzled nautical friend propounds the question: " How do those tiny spiders get on my yacht when I am twenty miles at sea? They could not have hatched simultaneously all over the ship, and I find them by the dozens all over the sails and rigging, and even on my clothing." I have heard of a little girl who ran in-doors to her mother in great excitement to tell her that it was "snowin' 'pider-webs," a picturesque and true statement as far as it goes, but which tells but half the story, for each of the falling webs held a pretty secret. What that secret was my yachtsman can readily guess, for the two half-stories taken together complete the tale. Various accounts of these gossamer showers have been handed down in history, and were always a mystery. Even the ancient Pliny records a "rain of wool," a phenomenon which, in a greater or less degree, is to be seen by every walker in the country during the late summer and autumn months—the annual picnic of the "ballooning spiders," whose peculiar aeronautic methods are shown in my illustration.

Gilbert White, in his "History of Selborne," written over a hundred years ago, gives a most graphic account of one of these cobweb showers:

"On September the 21st, 1741," he says, "being then on a visit, and intent on field diversions, I rose before daybreak. When I came into the enclosures, I found the stubbles and clover grounds matted all over with a thick coat of cobweb, in the meshes of which a copious and heavy dew hung so plentifully that the whole face of the country seemed as it were covered with two or three setting-nets drawn one over another. When the dogs attempted to hunt, their eyes were so blinded and hoodwinked that they could not proceed, but were obliged to lie down and scrape off the encumbrances from their faces with their fore feet, so that finding my sport interrupted, I returned home musing on the oddness of the occurrence. . . . About nine o'clock an appearance very unusual began to demand my attention—a shower of cobwebs falling from very elevated regions, and continuing without any interruption until the close of day. These webs are not single filmy threads floating in the air in all directions, but perfect flakes or rags, some near an inch broad and five or six long, which fell with a degree of velocity that showed they were considerably heavier than the atmosphere. On every side, as the observer turned his eyes, he might behold a continual succession of fresh flakes falling into his sight, and twinkling like stars as they turned their sides to the sun."

This same shower was witnessed by others, and one observer noted a similar one from the summit of a high mountain, the sky above him to the limit of his vision glistening with the silvery flakes.

White adds, further: "Strange and superstitious as were the notions about gossamers formerly, nobody in these days doubts that they are the real production of small spiders, which swarm in the fields in fine weather in autumn, and have a power of *shooting out webs from their tails*, so as to render themselves buoyant and lighter than the air."

I have italicized a phrase which is most suggestive, for such is the actual resource of the spider balloonist, a feat which may be witnessed by any one at the expense of a little trouble and patience.

Almost any bright autumn or late summer day is certain to reward our search—indeed, a search will hardly be necessary. The entire meadows are often draped in the glistening meshes. They festoon the grass tips, and wave their silken streamers from every mullein or other tall weed. Our garments are soon faced with a new warp and woof of glistening silk, and an occasional tickling betrays the floating fluffy mass which has encombed our hands or face. The glistening "rain of wool" of Pliny, or the mimic snow-squall of Gilbert White, I have witnessed many times, only in less degree, over the October rowen-fields.

This tickling upon our hands is perhaps not all to be accounted for by the mere contact of the silky web. If we examine closely, we shall doubtless find a lively little spider extricating itself from its unsatisfactory anchorage, and creeping to the nearest available position for a new flight. Even as you are examining the web upon your hand the spry midget has mounted to the top of your finger, and is off on his new silken balloon in a twinkling, sailing upward and out of sight even while his fellow-aeronauts are falling right and left. For this flying-machine, though a toy, as it were, of the wind, is still under control of the wise little sailor at the helm.

Almost any one of these flying tufts intercepted on our finger or upon a small stick will induce its little aeronaut to make a new start, and a careful examination with a pocket magnifier will disclose his secret. No matter how slight the breeze, he seems instantly to head against it, the abdomen is then raised, and in a moment a tiny stream of flossy glistening silk is seen issuing from the spinnerets beneath. Not the ordinary single web which we all know, but a broad band which represents the many hundreds of strands usually combined in the single thread, but now permitted to issue singly from the spinnerets. White speaks of the spider "shooting out" the web, and such is the apparent feat, but doubtless the breeze assists in the operation. It is certainly taking good care of this floating banner from the loom of this little spinner upon our finger-tip. Longer and longer it grows. A yard or more of its length is soon swaying about in the breeze. So buoyant has it now become that the little spider is visibly drawn upward, and now clings barely by his tip-toes. In another second he is off on his travels, where few could follow him even if they would. But this we *must* do if we would see the true "balloon," with its basket and rigging and captain all in perfect sailing trim.

Up to the point of ascension—to utter a Hibernianism—I have often thus followed my balloonist, but at this point I willingly yield the pursuit to a more competent witness, one whose recognized fame as the historian of the whole spider fraternity needs no emphasis from me. They have kept very few of their secrets from the Rev. Dr. McCook. He has followed them even in their flight, and has brought back all the tricks of their navigation. To have been able to describe as an eye-witness not only the ascension, but the subsequent alert and skilful rigging, trimming of ship, sailing, reefing, and final anchoring in port of this aeronaut with the silken jib, as Dr. McCook has done, acquiring his facts through a wild pantomime in the meadows, which for a time risked his reputation for sanity, is a triumph of patient investigation which deserves conspicuous acknowledgment.

Here is what the doctor observed while his

neighbors, as he ran cross-eyed over the meadow, were bewailing the loss of his reason:

"The spider, as she was raised from the perch, had her head downward. She immediately and swiftly reverses her position, clambers up her floating threads, at the same time throwing out a few filaments, which are cunningly twisted into a sort of basket into which the feet can rest. Now the upper legs grasp the lower of the ray, and the spinnerets, being released therefrom, are again set to work, and with amazing rapidity spin out a second and similar ray, which floats up behind her. Thus our aeronaut's balloon is complete, and she sits in the middle of it, drifting whither the breeze may carry her. She is not wholly at the mercy of the wind, however, for if she wishes to alight, she can gather the threads into a little white ball under her jaws; as they gradually shorten, the spider, having nothing to buoy her, sinks by her own weight, and the striking upon some elevated object, or falling upon the grass, makes her feel at home."

Having once alighted, the little pioneer immediately sets up house-keeping for herself, and the locality of its web in a year hence will doubtless be the scene of a similar balloon ascension, multiplied perhaps a thousandfold, from the neighborhood of a tuft of eggs somewhere concealed among the herbage—perhaps a brown, cocoon-like affair like that of the *Argiope riparia*, hung with its guy threads upon a dried fern.

The ballooning or flying spiders are not confined to any particular species. It seems to be an instinct with them all, but especially with the orb-weavers, or geometrical web-makers, and the wolf spiders; those queer short-legged specimens which dodge about upon the walls and fences, running forward or backward as the whim takes them, or even sideways in a manner at which a crab might turn green with envy.

A shower of cobwebs of unusual extent fell in the vicinity of Brooklyn about ten years ago, having been especially noted by a party of surveyors in Prospect Park, among whom was a noted scientist and naturalist. The ground was covered with the webs, averaging as many as fifteen to the square foot. The shower was later noticed by the same observers upon the summit of the Brooklyn Bridge tower, and doubtless covered several miles in area.

The Lace-Wing Fly

LACE indeed! Was ever lace even of fairy queen fashioned so daintily as are the wings of this diaphanous pale green sylph, that flutters in its filmy halo above the grass tips? Yonder it alights upon the clover. Let us steal closely upon its haunt. Here we find it hid under the upper leaf, its eyes of fiery gold gleaming in the shadow, its slender body now caged within the canopy of its four steep, sloping wings, their glassy meshes lit with iridescent hues of opal—the lace-wing fly, a delight to the eye, but whose fragile being is guarded from our too rude approach by a challenge to our sense of smell, which plainly warns us, " Touch not, handle not!" Our first capture of the fairy insect is always a memorable feat, with its lingering, odorous reminders, which not even soap and hot water will entirely obliterate from our finger-tips. But why should we have caught her? What an opportunity we threw away in her capture! Why not, rather, have followed the gauzy sprite, and learned something of her ways, something of the mission she is performing as she flits from leaf to leaf? For this is no idle flight of the lace-wing fly as we see her in the summer meadow. Her golden eyes are on a sharp lookout for a certain quest, and we are fortunate if we chance to surprise her softly at the time of her discovery, and with breathless stillness encourage her in the fulfilment of her plans. Everywhere among the grasses, weeds, and bushes we find the airy tokens of her visits; those delicate, hair-like fringes surrounding culm or twig, or growing like a tiny tuft of some webby mould upon the surface of leaf. But who even guesses the nature of the pretty fringe, or even associates with it the pale green golden-eyed fly which we all know so well?

Here beneath our close leaf is an opportunity which we must not permit to pass. Even as we take another cautious peep we discover that a cobwebby hair has grown from the surface of the leaf, with its tiny knob at the summit; and now another is growing beside it, following the pointed rising tip of the insect's slender tail. It has now reached a half-inch in length, when the little knob suddenly appears and is firmly glued to the summit of the hair. Another and another are added to the group, until a complete tuft or fringe hangs beneath the leaf. Of course the reader will have now guessed the secret of the episode—that this is a mother lace-wing fly thinking only of her future brood. But what a unique method she employs in egg-laying! What seeming reckless consideration for her offspring! Fancy awakening from one's crib only to find one's self on the top of a telegraph pole, or clinging for dear life at the end of a dangling rope or rod! Yet such is the initial experience of the baby lace-wing flies as they emerge from their filmy, iridescent cradles, whose very first experience in life must needs be a daring feat of acrobatics. But hunger is a mighty incentive to work and daring deeds, and the lace-wing infant is born hungry, grows hungrier with each moment of its subsequent life, and is apparently the more famished in proportion to its gluttony, fully realizing the comment of Josh Billings upon the voracious billy-goat, "All it eats seems tew go tew apetight."

We may be sure that this gauzy mother-fly, with her appetizing reminiscences of her former epicurean days, has placed her progeny in a land of plenty—a land almost literally of "milk and honey." For wherever we find this delicate fringe of pale green eggs we may confidently look also for its counterpart—a swarm of aphides, or plant-lice, somewhere in the neighborhood, occasionally clustering about the very stalks of the eggs, and shedding their copious "honey-dew" for the benefit of the caressing ants, which sip at their upraised, flowing pipes. Ah! if these happy ants only realized the menace of this slender fringe — who knows but that they may? — how quickly they were to be cut down by the destroying teeth!

Here, for instance, a wee babe just out of the egg slides down the stalk, and falls plump among a whole family of the aphides. In a twinkling a young aphis larger than himself is impaled on his sharp teeth and its body sucked dry. But this is merely an appetizer; he has only to extend his jaws on right or left to secure another similar morsel, which is emptied in the same manner, and his first meal would only seem to be limited by the number of victims available, so insatiate is his craving. In a short time he must needs move up farther along the twig, and thus his swath extends, until within an incredibly short space of time the entire swarm of aphides has disappeared, leaving the field occupied alone by the larva, who has perhaps now acquired his full growth by their absorption—a full-fledged "aphis lion," as he is called. He is now about a half-inch in length, a long pointed oval in outline, the sides of its body beset with bristly warts, and its head armed with two long incurved teeth. But these teeth are not like ordinary teeth, constructed for "chewing" or biting, but rather for imbibing, and suggest the two straws in the glass of the convivialist; being tubular, their open points are imbedded within the juicy body of the aphis, which is soon emptied to the last drop.

The aphides are always with us. Where is the lover of the rose-garden who is not painfully familiar with the pests, their pale green swarms completely encircling the tender shoots, and shedding their sticky, shining "honey-dew" everywhere like a varnish upon the leaves and flowers beneath. Hardly a plant or tree escapes their parasitic attacks in one form or another, where, with their beaks imbedded in the tender bark,

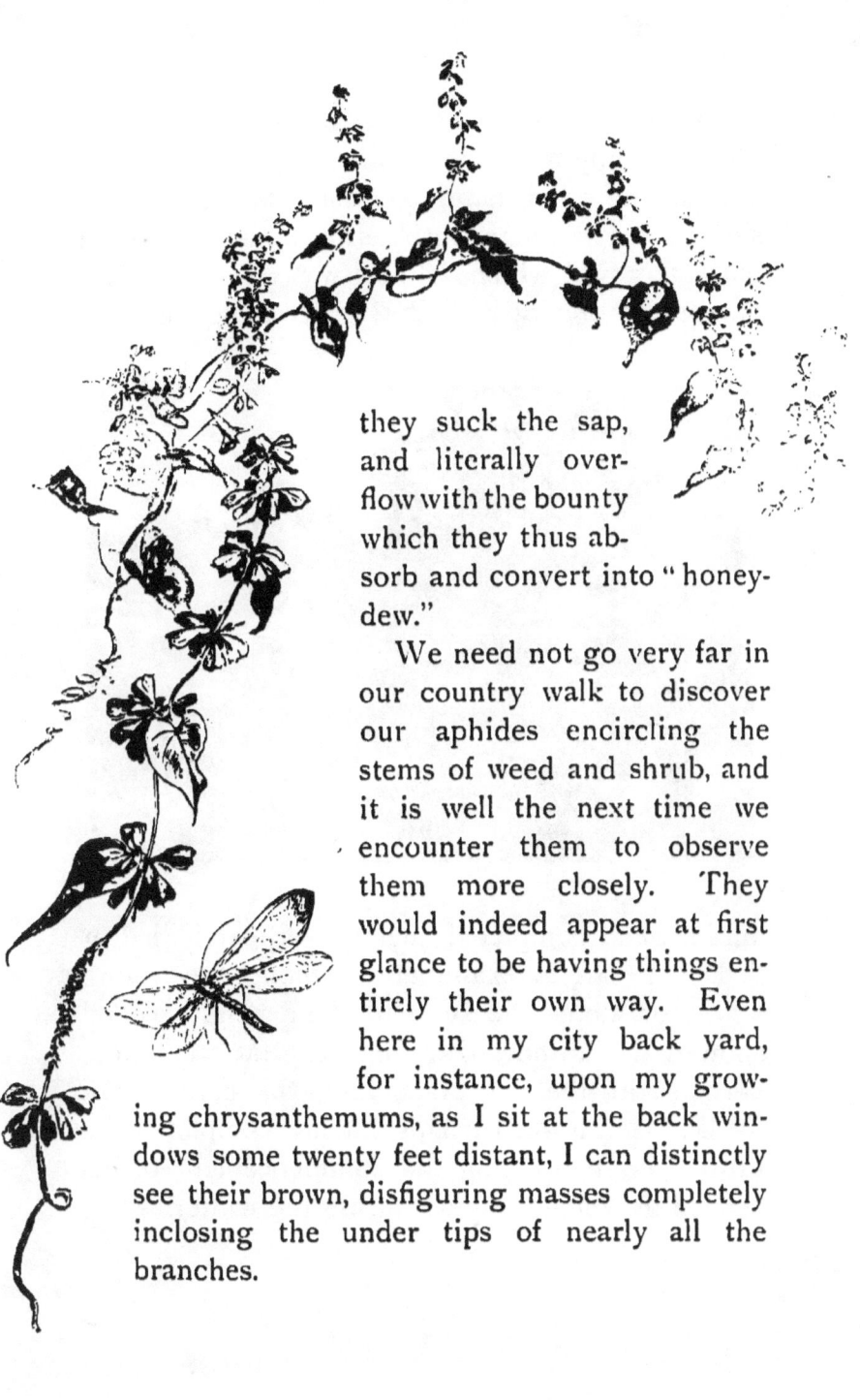

they suck the sap, and literally overflow with the bounty which they thus absorb and convert into "honey-dew."

We need not go very far in our country walk to discover our aphides encircling the stems of weed and shrub, and it is well the next time we encounter them to observe them more closely. They would indeed appear at first glance to be having things entirely their own way. Even here in my city back yard, for instance, upon my growing chrysanthemums, as I sit at the back windows some twenty feet distant, I can distinctly see their brown, disfiguring masses completely inclosing the under tips of nearly all the branches.

Again and again have I shaken or brushed them off only to see them increase and multiply; and, on the other hand, on more than one occasion have I seen an entire swarm vanish from a particular twig which I knew was infested only a day or two previous. Why? It was not that the

aphides had completed their growth and died or fled. A careful examination among the young leaves or along the stem in their neighborhood showed the author of the havoc, a fat aphis lion, perhaps, in the act of sucking the contents of its last victim, or, perhaps, having completed his growth, contemplating the commencement of his cocoon in which to abide during the winter.

Almost any swarm of aphides will show us this fat wolf in the fold, and if not this particular one, another—perhaps two others—quite as voracious, one of them the fat larva of the lady-bug, and the other a tapering-looking grub with needle beak and insatiable hunger, the larva of the gold-banded flower-fly.

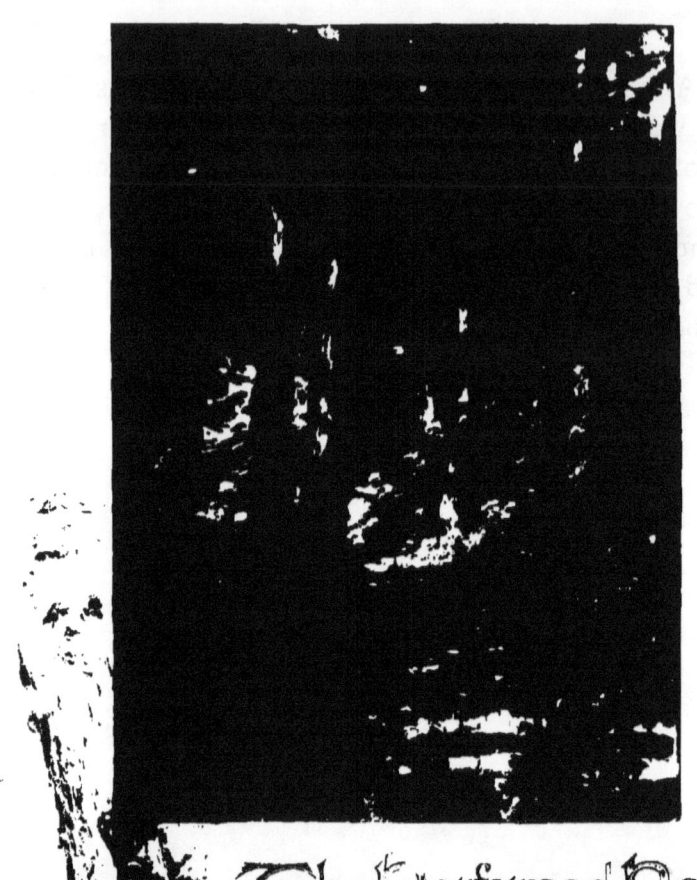

The Perfumed Beetle

SURPRISES await us at every turn in wood and field if our senses are sufficiently alert and responsive. I well remember the singular revelation which rewarded my curiosity upon a certain occasion in my boyhood, an incident which now seems trivial enough, but which marked a rare day in my youthful entomological education, and which, as it relates to an insect of exceptional peculiarity, I may here recall.

I was returning homeward after a successful day of hide-and-seek with the caterpillars and butterflies and beetles, my well-stored collecting-box being filled with squirming and creeping specimens, and my hat brim adorned with a swarm of Idalias, Archippus, yellow swallow-tails, and other butterflies—the butterfly-net on this particular occasion being rendered further useless by the occupancy of a big red adder which I wished to preserve "alive and sissin'." I had taken a short cut through the woods, and had paused to rest on a well-known mossy rock. The welcome odors of the woods, the mould, the dank moss, and the spice-bush lingered about me; and I well remember the occasional whiff from the fragrant pyrolas somewhere in my neighborhood, though unseen. It was a very warm day in the middle of July, and even the busiest efforts of millions of cool, fluttering leaves of the shadowed woods had barely tempered the languid breeze, laden as it was with the reminders of the glaring hay-field just outside its borders.

Among all the various odorous waftings that

came to me, I caught a whiff which was entirely new, and which in its suggestions seemed strangely out of place here in the woods. What was it like? It certainly reminded me of *something* with which my nostril was familiar, but which I could not now identify. I only knew that it had no place here in the woods, and even as I sought to take one extra full sniff for further analysis, it was gone. After the lapse of a few moments, however, its faint suggestion returned, and, increasing moment by moment, at length seemed to tincture the air like incense. It was now so strong as to be pungent, and my wits were keyed to their utmost, until at length a vision of a banana peel seemed to hover against the dried leaves. "Some one has been eating a banana here, and thrown the peel away," thought I. But no, this is hardly the odor of banana, either; it is more like pineapple. Yes, it *is* pineapple. No, that is not quite it either; it is strawberry. "Nonsense. Strawberry season was passed two weeks ago." And while I am debating the matter the spice-bush at my elbow has sent out a pungent challenge which has chased the enchantment all away. The next time it returns in a new guise, and the only suggestion which it brings is a reminder of my mother's red leather travelling-bag. Russia-leather? Yes, that is it—Russia-leather. No. Russia-leather, pineapple, strawberry, and banana peel mixed.

Whatever it was and wherever it came from I now determined to discover. The direction of the breeze was soon ascertained, and I started out to follow up the scent like a hound. I had walked about ten feet, with my nose tingling, when the odor suddenly left me. I paused at a large maple-tree, and awaited the trail. It came. This time it proved to be a hot scent, in truth. I needed only to follow my nose around the trunk of the tree at my elbow to be brought face to face with my game. It was no banana peel, nor pineapple, nor Russia-leather bag, but only a company of beetles sipping in the sun. A banquet of beetles! There were ten or a dozen of them, congregated about a hole in the maple trunk, all sipping at a furrow in the bark from which sap was oozing. At my approach they started to conceal themselves in the hole, but were most of them captured. They were about an inch in length, and of a purplish-brown color, and glistened like bronze.

I took my prizes home, and determined to announce my great discovery to the world in an early issue of some scientific paper, fully assured that I had made a "great find." Before accomplishing this purpose, however, I thought I would consult my "oracle," "Harris's Insects Injurious to Vegetation"—a most beautiful and valuable entomological work, by-the-way, which should be in every boy's library. There, on page forty-two, behold my odorous specimen, true to life! And what does Harris say about him? "They are nocturnal insects, and conceal themselves through the day in the crevices and hollows of trees, where they feed upon the sap that flows from the bark. They have the odor of Russia-leather, and give this out so powerfully that their presence can be detected by the scent alone at the distance of two or three yards from the place of their retreat. This strong smell suggested the name Osmoderma, 'scented skin,' given to these beetles by the French naturalists."

"Nocturnal" they may be, but that they are diurnal also I have many times proved. Almost any hot sunny day I am even now sure of my specimen upon a certain oozy cherry trunk near by, the presence even of one beetle being distinctly announced at a distance of ten feet.

There are two common species of these beetles, the present insect being the *Osmoderma scabei*, as given by Harris.

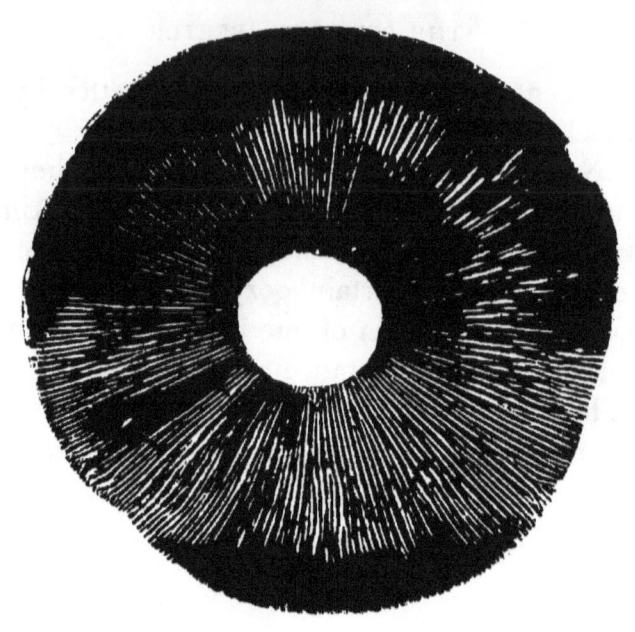

Mushroom Spore-prints

THE dusty puff-ball, floating its faint trail of smoke in the breeze from the ragged flue at its dome-shaped roof as from an elfin tepee, or perhaps enveloping our feet in its dense purple cloud as we chance to step upon it in the path, is familiar to every one —always enthusiastically welcomed by the small boy, to whom it is always a challenge for a kick, and a consequent demonstration of smoke worthy of a Fourth-of-July celebration.

A week ago this glistening gray bag, so free with its dust-puff at the slightest touch, was solid in substance and as white as cottage cheese in the fracture.

But in a later stage this clear white fracture would have appeared speckled or peppered with gray spots, and the next day entirely gray and much softened, and, later again, brown and apparently in a state of decay. But this is not *decay*. This moist brown mass becomes powdery by evaporation, and the puff-ball is now *ripe*, and intent only on posterity.

Each successive squeeze as we hold it between our fingers yields its generous response in a puff of brown smoke, which melts away apparently into air. But the puff-ball does not end in mere smoke. This vanishing purple cloud is composed of tiny atoms, so extremely minute as to require the aid of a powerful microscope to reveal their shapes. Each one of these atoms, so immaterial and buoyant as to be almost without gravity, floating away upon the slightest breath, or even wafted upward by currents of warm air from the heated earth, has within itself the power of reproducing another clump of puff-balls if only fortune shall finally lodge it in congenial soil. These spores are thus analogous to the seeds of ordinary plants. We have seen the myriadfold dispersion of its potential atoms in the cloud of spore-smoke from the puff-ball, but who ever thinks of a spore-cloud from a mushroom or a toadstool? Yet the same method is followed by all the other fungi, but with less conspicuousness. The puff-ball gives a visible salute, but any one of the common mushrooms or toadstools will afford us a much prettier and more surprising account of itself if we but give it the opportunity. This big yellow toadstool out under the poplar-tree, its golden cap studded with brownish scurfy warts, its under surface beset with closely plaited laminæ or gills, who could ever associate the cloud of dry smoke with this moist, creamy-white surface? We may sit here all day and watch it closely, but we shall see no sign of anything resembling smoke or dust. But even so, a filmy mist is continually floating away from beneath its golden cap, the eager breeze taking such jealous care of the continual shower that our eyes fail to perceive a hint of it.

Do you doubt it? You need wait but a few moments for a proof of the fact in a pretty experiment, which, when once observed, will certainly be resorted to as a frequent pastime in leisure moments when the toadstool or mushroom is at hand.

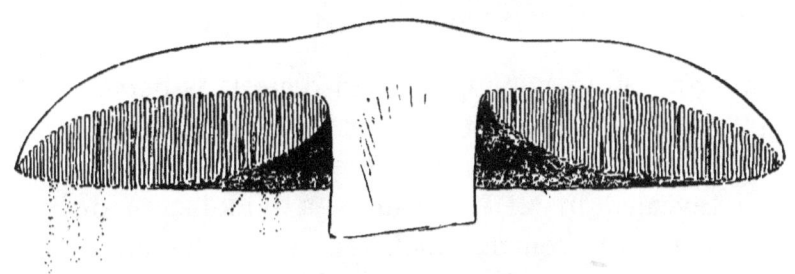

Spore Surface of a Polyporus

Here is a very ordinary-looking specimen growing beside the stone steps at our back door perhaps. Its top is gray; its gills beneath are fawn-color. We may shake it as rudely as we will, and yet we shall get no response such as the puff-ball will give us. But let us lay it upon a piece of white paper, gills downward, on the mantel, and cover it with a tumbler or finger-bowl, so as to absolutely exclude the least admission of air. At the expiration of five minutes, perhaps, we may detect a filmy, pinkish-yellow tint on the paper, following beneath the upraised border of the cap, like a shadow faintly lined with white. In a

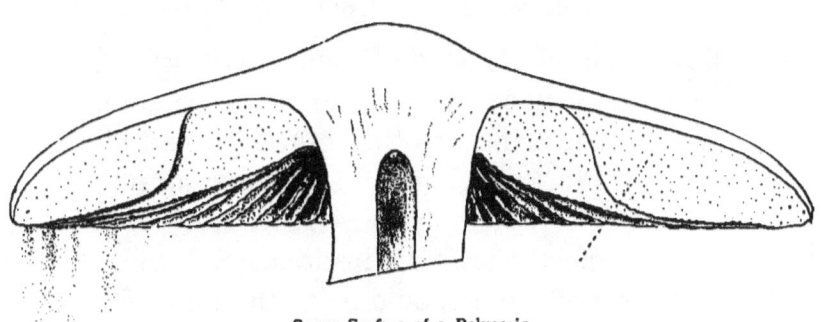

Spore Surface of a Polygaric

quarter of an hour the tinted deposit is perceptible across the room; and in an hour, if we carefully raise the mushroom, the perfect spore-print is revealed in all its beauty—a pink-brown disk with a white centre, which represents the point of contact of the cut stem, and white radiating lines, representing the edges of the thin gills, many of them as fine and delicate as a cobweb.

Every fresh species will yield its surprise in the markings and color of the prints.

These spore-deposits are of course fugitive, and will easily rub off at the slightest touch. But inasmuch as many of these specimens, either from their beauty of form or exquisite color, or for educational or scientific purposes, it will be desirable to preserve, I append simple rules for the making of the prints by a process by which they will become effectually "fixed," and thus easily kept without injury.

DIRECTIONS FOR MAKING A MUSHROOM SPORE-PRINT

Take a piece of smooth white writing-paper and coat its surface evenly with a thin solution of gum-arabic, dextrine, or other mucilage, and allow it to dry. Pin this, gummed side uppermost, to a board or table, preferably over a soft cloth, so that it will lie perfectly flat. To insure a good print the mushroom specimen should be fresh and firm, and the gills or spore-surface free from breaks or bruises.

Cut the stem off about level with the gills, then lay the mushroom, spore-surface downward, upon the paper, and cover with a tumbler, finger-bowl, or other vessel with a smooth, even rim, to absolutely exclude the slightest ingress of air.

After a few hours have passed by, perhaps even less, the spores will be seen through the glass on the paper at the extreme edge of the mushroom, their depth of color indicating the density of the deposit. If we now gently lift the glass, and with the utmost care remove the fungus, perhaps by the aid of pins previously inserted, in a *perfectly vertical* direction, without the slightest side motion, the spore-print in all its beauty will be revealed—perhaps a rich brown circular patch with exquisite radiating white lines, marking the direction and edges of the gills, if an Agaric; perhaps a delicate pink, more or less clouded disk, here and there distinctly and finely honey-combed with white lines, indicating that our specimen is one of the polypores, as a Boletus. Other prints will yield rich golden disks, and there will be prints of red, lilac, greens, oranges, salmon-pinks, and browns and purples, variously lined in accordance with the number and nature of the gills or pores. Occasionally we shall look in vain for our print, which may signify that our specimen had already scattered its spores ere we had found it, or, what is more likely, that the spores are *invisible* upon the paper, owing to their whiteness, in which case a piece of black paper must be substituted for the white ground, when the response will be beautifully manifest in a white tracery upon the black background. One of these, from the *Amanita muscarius*, is reproduced in our illustration. If the specimen is left too long, the spore-deposit is continued upward between the gills, and may reach a quarter of an inch in height, in which case, if extreme care in lifting the cap is used, we observe a very realistic counterfeit of the gills of the mushroom in high relief upon the paper. A print of this kind is of course very fragile, and must be handled with care. But a comparatively slight deposit of the spores, without apparent thickness, will give us the most perfect print, while at the same time yielding the full color. Such a

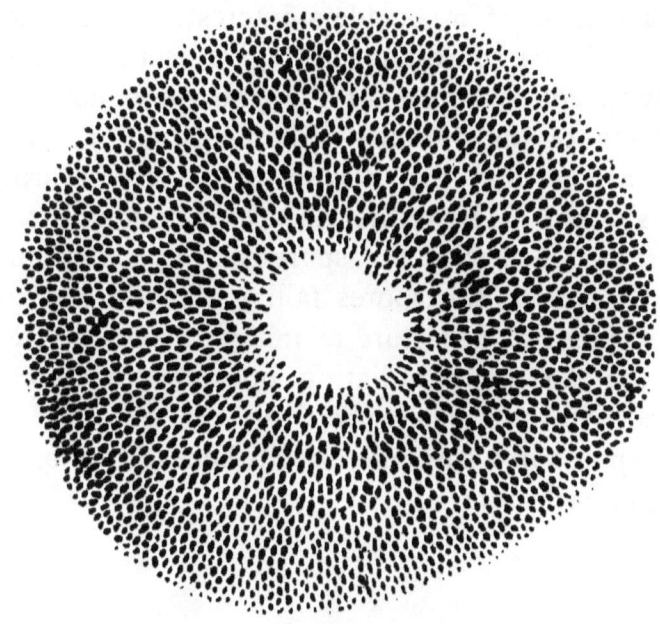

print may also be fixed by our present method so as to withstand considerable rough handling, all that is required being to lay the print upon a wet towel until the moisture has penetrated through the paper and reached the gum. The spores are thus set, and, upon drying the paper, are quite securely fixed. Indeed, the moisture often exuded by the confined fungus beneath the glass proves sufficient to dampen the mucilage and set the spores.

A number of prints may be obtained from a single specimen.

To those of my readers interested in the science of this spore-shower I give sectional illustrations of examples of the two more common groups of mushrooms — the Agaric, or gilled mushroom, and the Polyporus, or tube-bearing mushroom. The entire surface of both gills and pores is lined with the spore-bearing membrane, or hymenium, the spores falling directly beneath their point of departure as indicated; in the case of the Agaric, in radiating lines in correspondence with the spaces between the gills, and in Polyporus in a tiny pile directly beneath the opening of each pore.

Some Curious Cocoons

THE title of this article will doubtless recall to readers of "Harper's Young People"* a paper upon a similar subject which appeared in my calendar series two years ago. With the title the resemblance ends, for the cocoons which I am about to describe are of a sort that has never been mentioned in any previous article. These curious cocoons had been familiar to me since my boyhood, having long excited my wonder before finally revealing their mystery. They have recently been brought freshly to my notice by a letter that I have received, accompanied by a box of specimens, which reads as follows:

* Now "Harper's Round Table."

Dear Mr. Gibson,—I have sent you to-day what I take to be three cocoons. These with three others I picked up from a gravel-walk in Po'keepsie over a year ago. They seemed connected at the ends, but easily broke apart. I kept them, purposing to see what would emerge, but nothing has rewarded my watch, and they seem now to be shrivelling up. Can you give me any information in regard to them? If so, I shall be very grateful to you.

I had barely read half through the brief description when I guessed the nature of the cocoons in question, having received similar letters before, as well as verbal queries, from others who had been puzzled by the non-committal specimens. The fact that they were found "on the gravel-walk," and were loosely "connected at the ends," was in itself strong evidence of their questionable nature, and I felt sure that I should recognize the cocoons as old friends. And I did.

Upon opening the box, I found three of them packed in a mass of cotton, two of them still loosely attached at the ends, the third one somewhat disintegrated. Each was about an inch in length, and half an inch in thickness, somewhat egg or cocoon shaped. Upon being separated, one end of each was seen to be hollowed out, and had thus previously received the pointed end of its fellow in the "connected" condition in which they had been found. In color they were a mouse gray precisely, and to the careless observer might have appeared to consist of caterpillar silk, though in reality having a substance more like felt. Yes, they might easily be mistaken for cocoons if we simply contented ourselves with looking at them.

Who, by a mere glance, could imagine the materials that the little bird called the vireo employs

in building her peculiar nest? The reader will remember how we pulled one of those nests apart, and what strange materials we found woven in its fabric.* But they were hardly more surprising than we may discover within this sly cocoon if we dissect it. Now, to begin with, a true cocoon is not solid to the core, as this one evidently is as we press it between our fingers, nor can you pinch off a tuft of gray hair from the sur-

* See "Sharp Eyes," page 220.

face of an ordinary cocoon when you will. True, there are some cocoons into whose silk meshes the caterpillar weaves the hair of its body, but the felt thus formed is only a shell, and is intermeshed with silken webs, and one pinch alone will open up the hollow interior and show us the caterpillar or chrysalis within. Such, for instance, is the little brown winter snuggery of the woolly-bear caterpillar which we all know, and whose prickly cocoons may be found beneath stones and logs in the fields.

But what do we find in these cocoons that we now have before us? Not only is there no vestige of silk to be seen, but there are hairs enough in this single cocoon to have supplied a hundred caterpillars, while we look in vain for any sign of the spinner within. Indeed, there is no within; pinch after pinch reveals nothing but the same gray felt. We are now a quarter of an inch below the surface, when another pinch brings with it a small mass of white specks like crumbs intermingled with the hair, and in the hollow thus deepened we observe a shiny white object like ivory, with a minute ball at its tip. It certainly looks like a tiny bone. We impatiently break open the cocoon, when we see in truth a bone—indeed, a compact mass of bones from some very small animal, whose identity we may guess from the mouse-color of the felt. Here is the femur of

a field-mouse—two of them—also a part of the fibula, and a dozen or more other bones. Breaking asunder the mass further, we find a few tiny teeth; and as we continue the process in the remaining two specimens, we bring to light parts of the skull, ribs, and vertebræ. A strange "cocoon" indeed.

A further examination of the remaining specimens disclosed similar ingredients, until the entire mass presented a collection somewhat like that shown in my illustration.

I well remember my first encounter with the queer specimens, and what mysteries they were, though the "cocoon" idea had never suggested itself to me, the felted mass having been found in

a disintegrated state.

It was on a winter's day, in a walk on the crusted snow, during my early boyhood. Returning by the brink of a stream, I noticed a little gray mass of fur on the snow, which on examination disclosed numerous bones of what I took to be field-mice and parts of the anatomy of a mole intermingled with the hair. No vestige of flesh appeared in the mass, and I fell to wondering what manner of disease is this with which the mouse world is afflicted that should consume the flesh and leave nothing but a disjointed skeleton and a tiny pile of fur. Ah, had I only known then what I discovered a year or two later—the secret of that big hollow in the willow-tree above—my little pile of fur and bones would easily have been explained, for there summer after summer sat the little brown screech-owl, blinking in the sun at her doorway, peeping through the tiny cracks of her closed eyelids at noon, and at midnight commanding a view of the entire surrounding sedgy swamp in her eager quest for the first unfortunate shrew or deer-mouse that should peep its nose out of its nest or venture across the ice in the field of her staring vision.

The new-fallen snow would doubtless show as many telltales of midnight tragedies among the little bead-eyed folk—the tiny trail terminating in a drop of blood, and a suggestive ruffling of the surrounding snow, with its plain witness of the fatal swoop of "owl on muffled wing" from its vantage-ground here in the willow-tree. To-night our little deer-mouse ventured too far from its nest among the tussocks. To-morrow night all that will be left of its sprightly squeaking identity will be a tiny pile of fur and bones disgorged in the form of pellets from the open beak of the owl on the willow-tree.

In regard to these specimen pellets which my correspondent has sent to me for identification,

I am not prepared to affirm that they are from the digestive laboratory of the owl. Something in their size suggests that a hawk is equally likely to be responsible for them, all the birds of prey having this same singular habit of ejecting the indigestible portions of animals which they devour. A pet red-tailed hawk which I kept during the past summer littered its pen with pellets of a similar size and consistency to these, varied on one occasion with a number composed entirely of grass, which explained a singular puzzle of the day previous, when I descried my hawk with its craw largely distended, and wondered what squirrel or chipmonk or snake had been thus caught napping in my absence.

NETTLE-LEAF
TENT-BUILDERS

VERY few of our readers will need an introduction to the nettle. It is, perhaps, the one plant which may claim the largest number of intimate acquaintances. It was Dr. Culpepper, the old-time herbalist, I believe, who claimed, moreover, that it was one of the easiest of plants to distinguish, in proof of which he affirmed that "it could be found even on the darkest night by simply feeling for it." Even those most ignorant of botany, after having once "scraped acquaintance," as it were, with the nettle, find it to their interest to keep its memory green.

It is partly because it *is* so well known, and partly because so few people use their eyes analytically, that a certain little mystery of the plant is so well guarded. For almost any bed of nettles may well tempt the young entomologist to tarry, while he forgets the tingling fingers as he fills his collecting-box with welcome specimens.

We are sure to have company if we linger long about our nettles. There is a small brood of butterflies which we can always count upon. Here is one of them coming over the meadow. It has a sharp eye for nettles, and is even now on the lookout for them. In a moment more its beautiful black, scarlet-bordered and white-spotted wings are seen fluttering among the leaves, alighting now here, now there, each brief visit leaving a visible witness if we care to look for it. It has now settled upon a leaf within easy reach. Creeping along its edge, it is soon hanging beneath, but only for a second, and is off again on the wing. Let us pluck the leaf. Upon looking beneath it we may see the pretty token of the Red Admiral, a tiny egg which we may well preserve for our microscope.

We shall not wait long before another butterfly visitor arrives, smaller than the last, and with its deep orange, black-spotted wings conspicuously jagged at the edges—one of the "angle-wings," which immediately announces his name as he alights with wings folded close above his back, disclosing the silver "comma" in the midst of the dull brown of the nether surface. Many are the tiny tokens which she also leaves behind her as she flutters away in search of a new nettle-clump.

We have been closely observing these two butterflies perhaps for half an hour, and during that time our eyes have rested a dozen times upon a condition of things here among the leaves which certainly should have immediately arrested our attention. Almost within touch of our hand, upon one stalk, are three leaves which certainly do not hang like their fellows. One of them has been drawn up at the edges, and fully one-half of its lower portion is gone, while its angle of drooping indicates more than the mere weight of the leaf. "A spider's nest, of course," you remark. As such it has been passed a thousand times even by young and enthusiastic entomological students who would have risked their lives for a "cecropia" or a "bull's-eye" caterpillar, or stung their hands mercilessly as they swept their butterfly net among those very stinging leaves. It is interesting to gather a few of these "spider's nests," and examine the cause of their heavy droop, which proves to be a healthy-looking gray caterpillar an inch or more in length, covered with formidable spines, perpetuating as it were the tendency of its foster-

plant. Only yesterday he built himself this tent, having abandoned the remnant tent just below, for he eats himself out of house and home every couple of days. About five weeks ago he began his career, his first meal consisting, perhaps, of the iridescent shell of a tiny egg—precisely such a one as our first butterfly visitor has just left, for this is the caterpillar of the Atalanta or Red Admiral.

We may find a number of these tents if we look sharp, and even while gathering them may overlook a still more remarkable roof-tree of another caterpillar, which constructs its pavilion on quite a different plan. This, too, might even deceive a "spider," the edges of the leaves being drawn together *beneath*, and the veins partly severed near the stem, giving it quite a steep pitch. Upon looking beneath, we disclose another prickly tenant somewhat similar to the first, only that he is yellow and black instead of gray, while he is clothed with the same complementary growth of branching spines.

A single nettle-clump of any size will disclose dozens, perhaps hundreds, of these tent-dwellers. Though armed with formidable *chevaux-de-frise*, these species are stingless, and the caterpillars may be safely gathered. The object of my directing attention to them is not simply to disclose them in their haunts, but to recommend their transfer to our collecting-box, looking to the further beautiful surprise—always a surprise—which they have in store for us. Although they quickly desert their tents in captivity, they continue to feed on the fresh leaves provided from day to day, and suffer little in confinement.

The full-grown caterpillars are about an inch and a half in length, and if our specimens average such dimensions we shall not have many days to wait for our surprise. Perhaps to-morrow, as we open the lid of our box, the caterpillars will be seen to have left the leaves, and to be scattered here and there on the lid or walls of their prison in apparent listlessness. Let us observe this individual here beneath the box cover. Its body is bent in a curve, and a careful inspection reveals a carpet of glistening silk, to which it clings. Now the insect regains confidence, and takes up the thread which it dropped a moment ago when the box was opened, its head moving from side to side in a motion suggesting a figure 8, with variations. Gradually, through the lapse of several minutes, this sweep is concentrated to a more central point, which is at length raised into a minute tuft of silk; and if we wait and watch for a few moments longer, we shall see our spinner turn about and clasp this tuft with its hinder pair of feet. And this same process has been going on in different parts of our box. Lifting the lid an hour or two later, we find the interior full of the caterpillars dangling by their tails, each with its body forming a loop.

Twenty-four hours after this suspension a singular feat and a beautiful transformation take place, a revelation which, as I have said, even to those already familiar with it, is always new and surprising. Here, indeed, may we observe "the miraculous in the common."

It is as though our box had met with some enchantment beneath the wand of Midas or Iris; for is it not, indeed, a box of jewels that is now disclosed, a treasury of quaint golden ear-drops of a fashioning unlike any to be seen in a show-case, but which might well serve as a rare model for the mimetic art of the jeweller? When we consider the length to which these exquisite artisans will go for their natural originals—the orchids in gems, beetles in jewelled enamel, butterflies in brilliants and emeralds and rubies—need we wonder that this one most significant model of nature's own jewelry, apparently designed as a tempting pendant, should have been ignored by a class of designers to whom its claims would seem irresistible? But we forget. The jeweller is not necessarily an entomologist or naturalist. The butterfly, the

beetle, the flower, every one sees; how few even dream of these glowing chrysalids (aurelias) which hang beneath the nettle leaves or in unseen coverts among the hop or thistle?

I have looked in vain among all the designs in the shops for any hint of the existence of such a thing as the aurelia of Archippus, comma, semicolon, Red Admiral, Hunters, White J.; and, indeed, even if wrought to imitative perfection, how few would recognize any resemblance to aught on the earth or in the waters under the earth!

I will not attempt to describe this living gem of our "comma." There are degrees in its brilliancy, an occasional specimen being almost a mass of gold. Indeed, we need scarce wonder that the aurelia should have proved so tempting a lure to the ancient alchemists.

Almost any group of nettles will show us our "comma" caterpillar, but one of its favorite haunts is the wood-nettle, a large-leaved, low variety, which is to be found in moist woods and shady river-banks, and will be recognized by the illustration on the preceding page. I have gathered many of these animated tented leaves in a few moments' search among the plants.

I have said nothing of the wonderful transformation of the caterpillar to its chrysalis, and the astonishing trick by which the latter gets out of its skin, and again catches the silken loop with its tail. This feat is well worth a close study; the authorities in the past have all been at sixes and sevens as to what really takes place. Which of our boys or girls can discover the facts as they *are*, and tell us why the chrysalis does not fall out at the last moment?

The Evening Primrose

THE summer which is allowed to pass without a visit to the twilight haunt of the evening primrose, perhaps at your very door, is an opportunity missed. Night after night for weeks it breathes its fragrant invitation as its luminous blooms flash out one by one from the clusters of buds in the gloom, as though in eager response to the touch of some wandering sprite, until the darkness is lit up with their luminous galaxy — that beautiful episode of blossom-consciousness and hope so picturesquely described by Keats:

> "A tuft of evening primroses
> O'er which the wind may hover till it dozes,
> O'er which it well might take a pleasant sleep,
> But that 'tis ever startled by the leap
> Of buds into ripe flowers."

Nor is it necessary to brave the night air to witness this sudden transformation. A cluster of the flowers placed in a vase beneath an evening lamp will reveal the episode, though robbed of the poetic attribute of their natural sombre environment and the murmuring response of the twilight moth, a companion to which its form, its color, and its breath of perfume and impulsive greeting are but the expression of a beautiful divine affinity.

Then there is that pretty daylight mystery of the faded, drooping bells of last night's impulsive blossoms, each perhaps tenanted by the tiny, faithful moth which first welcomed its open twilight chalice, and which now has crept close within its wilted cup, the yellow tips of its protruding wings simulating the fading petals. And again, a few weeks later, with what surprise do we discover that these long columns of green seed-pods are not always what they seem, but are intermingled with or supplanted by smooth, green caterpillars which exactly resemble them in size and general shape, the progeny of our tiny pink and yellow moth now feeding on the young seed-pods! Verily even a vireo or worm-eating warbler, who is supposed to know a green caterpillar when he sees one, might perch among these without a suspicion, except perhaps at the tickling of its feet by the rudely touched victim.

But these are not all the interesting features of the evening primrose. It has still another curious secret, which has doubtless puzzled many a country stroller, and which is suggested in the following inquiry from a rural correspondent:

"I read in 'Harper's Young People' your piece about the evening primrose, and found the little moth and the catterpilers, what I never seen before; but they is one thing what you never tole us about yit. Why is it that the buds on so meny evening primroses swell up so big and never open? Some of them has holes into them, but I never seen nothing cum out."

This same question must have been mentally propounded by many observers who have noted this singular peculiarity of the buds—two sorts of buds, one of them long and slender, and with a longer tube; the other short and stout, with no tube at all—both of which are shown in proper proportion in my illustration. It is well to contrast their outward form, and to note wherein they differ. In the normal or longer bud the tube is slender, and extended to a length of an inch or more, while in the shorter specimen this portion is reduced to about a fifth or sixth of that length, while the corolla enclosed within its sepals is much shortened and swollen.

The difference in the shape and development of these two buds is a most interesting study, as bearing upon the conscious intention of the flower as an embodiment of a divine companion to an insect. What is the intention involved in the construction and habit of this flower? Why this long tube? Why does it await the twilight to burst into bloom?

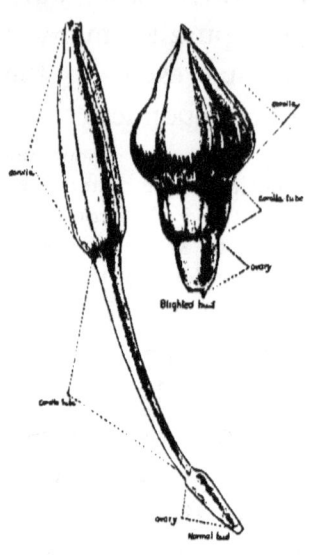

In the new botany of Darwin flowers must be considered as embodiments of welcome to insects. Long ago it was discovered that the powdery pollen of a flower must reach the stigma of the flower in order to produce seed. It was formerly supposed that this was naturally accomplished by the stamens shedding this pollen directly upon the stigma, but this was later shown to be impossible in most flowers, the anthers containing the pollen being so placed that they could not thus convey the pollen. This fact was first noted by Sprengel in 1735, who was the first to discover that the flower, with its color, perfume, and honey, was really designed to attract insects, and that only by their unconscious aid could the pollen be thus carried to the stigma. But Sprengel had supposed that the intention of the blossom was the reception of its *own* pollen, a fact which

was again soon seen to be impossible, as the stigmas of many flowers are closed when their own pollen is being shed. It remained for Darwin seventy years later to interpret the problem. Insects were intentionally attracted to the flower; but the pollen with which their bodies thus became dusted was designed to be carried to the stigmas of another flower, showing cross-fertilization to be the intention in nearly all blossoms.

The endless shapes of flowers were shown by Darwin to have reference to certain insects upon whom the flower depended for the transfer of its pollen. What are we to infer from the shape of our evening primrose? Its tube is long and slender, and the nectar is secreted at its farthest ex-

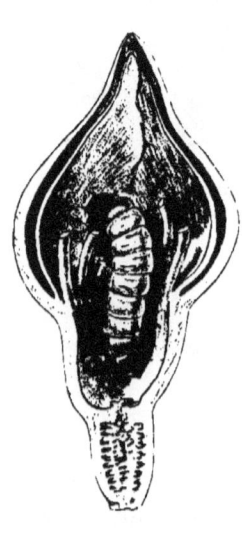

tremity. Only a tongue an inch or so in length could reach it. What insects have tongues of this length? Moths and butterflies. The primrose blooms at night, when butterflies are asleep, and is thus clearly adapted to moths. The flower opens; its stigma is closed; the projecting stamens scatter the loose pollen upon the moth as it sips close at the blossom's throat, and as it flies from flower to flower it conveys it to other blossoms whose stigmas are matured. The expression of the normal bud is thus one of affinity and hope.

Our friend just quoted mentions having seen "holes" on the other swollen buds, and there is certain to be a hole in every one of them at its maturity. But let us select one which is as yet entire. If with a sharp knife-point we cut gently through its walls, we disclose the curious secret of its abnormal shape—"the worm i' the bud," as shown in my accompanying sketch—and what an eloquent story of blighted hopes its interior condition reveals! This tiny whitish caterpillar which we disclose in the petal dungeon has been a prisoner since its birth, during the early growth of the bud. One by one the stamens and also the stigma have been devoured for food, until the mere vestiges of them now remain. With no stamens to bequeath pollen, and no stigma to welcome other pollen, what need to open? What need to elongate a corolla tube for the tongue of a moth whose visit could render no functional service?

So thus our blighted buds refuse to open, where blooming would be but a mockery. This tiny caterpillar has a host of evening primrose blossoms laid to his door. When full grown he is nearly a third of an inch in length, at which time he concludes to leave his life-long abode, which explains the "hole" through the base of the bud. If we gather a few of these buds and place them in a small box, we may observe the remaining life history of the insect. After creeping from its petal home it immediately spins a delicate white silken cocoon, and within a day or so changes to a chrysalis. At the expiration of about a fortnight, as we open the box, we are apt to liberate one or more tiny gray moths, which upon examination we are bound to confess are a poor recompense for the blossom for which they are the substitute.

This little moth is shown very much enlarged in the accompanying illustration. Its upper wings are variously mottled with gray and light brown, and thickly fringed at their tips, while the two lower wings are like individual feathers, fringed on both sides of a narrow central.

These and other characters ally the insect with the great group known as the *Tineidæ*, of which the common clothes moth is a notorious example.

The Dandelion Burglar

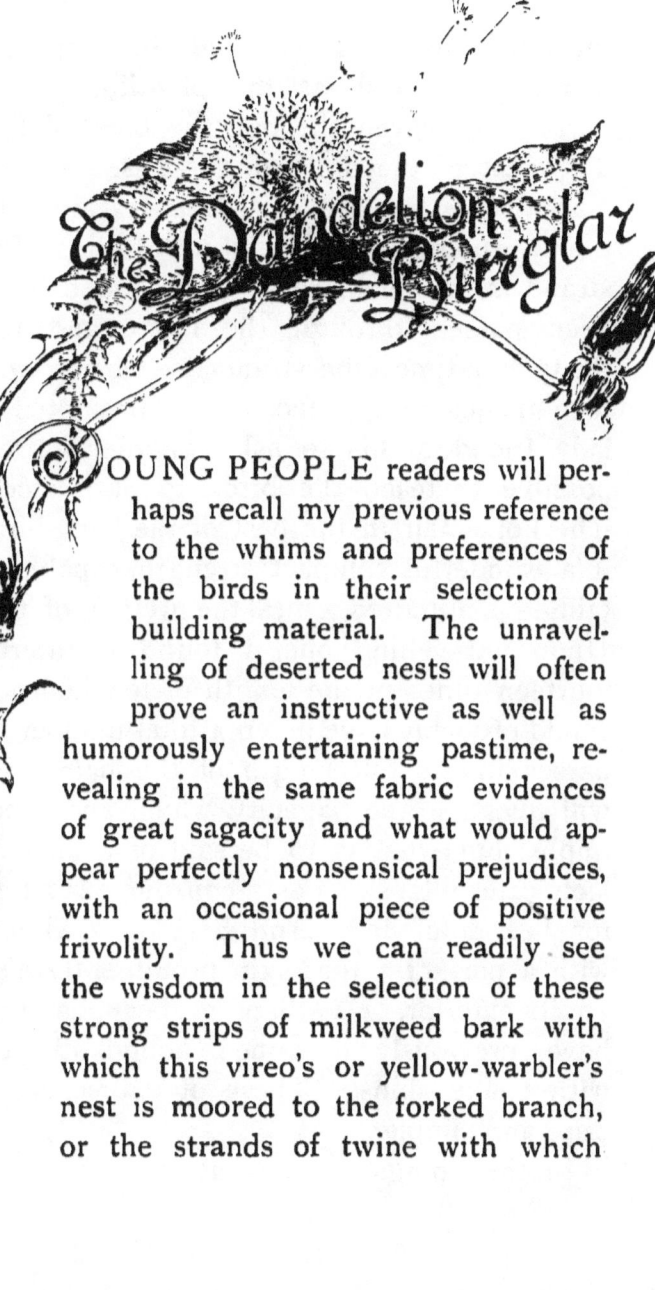

YOUNG PEOPLE readers will perhaps recall my previous reference to the whims and preferences of the birds in their selection of building material. The unravelling of deserted nests will often prove an instructive as well as humorously entertaining pastime, revealing in the same fabric evidences of great sagacity and what would appear perfectly nonsensical prejudices, with an occasional piece of positive frivolity. Thus we can readily see the wisdom in the selection of these strong strips of milkweed bark with which this vireo's or yellow-warbler's nest is moored to the forked branch, or the strands of twine with which the Baltimore oriole suspends its deep swinging hammock, as well as the plentiful meshing of horse-hair woven through the body of the nest. The nest of the orchard oriole is even more remarkable as a piece of woven texture. Wilson, the ornithologist, by careful unravelling of a grass strand from one of these nests, found it to have been passed through the fabric and returned thirty-four times, the strand itself being only thirteen inches long, a fact which prompted an old lady friend of his to ask "whether it would be possible to teach the birds to darn stockings." The horse-hair in the nest of the hang-bird gives it a wonderful compact strength, capable of sustaining a hundred times the weight of the bird. Upon unravelling one, I found it intermeshed fourteen times in the length of ten inches, which would probably have given a total number of forty passes in the full length of the hair. No one will question the sagacity which such materials imply; but what is to be said of a bird that selects caterpillar-skins as a conspicuous adornment for her domicile? And here is a vireo's nest with a part of a toad-skin prominently displayed on its exterior, or perhaps a specimen such as I have previously described abundantly covered with snake-skins. These, of course, are whims pure and simple.

In the linings of many nests we find an equal

variety, but the materials are selected with a definite purpose, a soft, warm bed for the young fledglings being the object sought by the parent birds. To this end we find many nests lined with what the ornithologists call "soft downy substances." Examination with a magnifying glass will sometimes show us precisely the nature of this down; whether it consists of wool from a sheep or hair from the deer, 'coon, goat, or horse; whether it is composed of fuzz from downy leaves or spiderwebs, caterpillar hairs, or cottony seeds of plants. These last form a favorite nest lining with a number of birds.

I remember once finding a beautiful nest of a warbler whose outer wall was strongly woven with strands of milk-weed bark, but the whole interior filled with a felt composed of dandelion seeds, and barely anything else. The nest was old and weather-beaten, and the mass had been reduced to a consistency resembling thick brown paper, with an occasional seed protruding. Originally this soft mass must have been at least a quarter of an inch in thickness. The dandelion seed is an occasional ingredient in many nests. We can readily understand how a bird with an eye to a downy snuggery for her young might be tempted to gather an occasional seed, but it takes a host of dandelion seeds to make a thick cushion such as this which I have mentioned, and we might well wonder at the labor involved in the accumulation of such a mass. A cloudy dandelion ball in the grass doubtless looks inviting to the nest-builder, but how much of this tuft would the bird be able to secure in her bill when a mere touch or breath perhaps is sufficient to scatter the ball to the breeze? No; I cannot believe my bird of the dandelion nest wasted her energies in picking up a single seed here and there from a dandelion ball, or perhaps on the wing. A discovery of a few years ago has shown me how dandelion seeds may be cleverly gathered by a shrewd nest-builder, and how a whole nest may be feathered with them without much labor.

For some years I was puzzled to account for a peculiar mutilation which I often observed on the dandelion. It was always at the same place—the calyx of the blossom—the green portion which incloses the bud, and, after blooming, closes again about the withered flower, and so remains while the seeds are growing. Most of my readers have seen dandelion flowers in all their stages of growth. The flower usually blooms for three mornings. By this time all the tiny yellow flowerets which make up the yellow cushion have bloomed. The green calyx now closes, to remain closed, for a week, while the stem generally bends outward, and thus draws the withered flower towards the ground, often hiding it beneath the leaves.

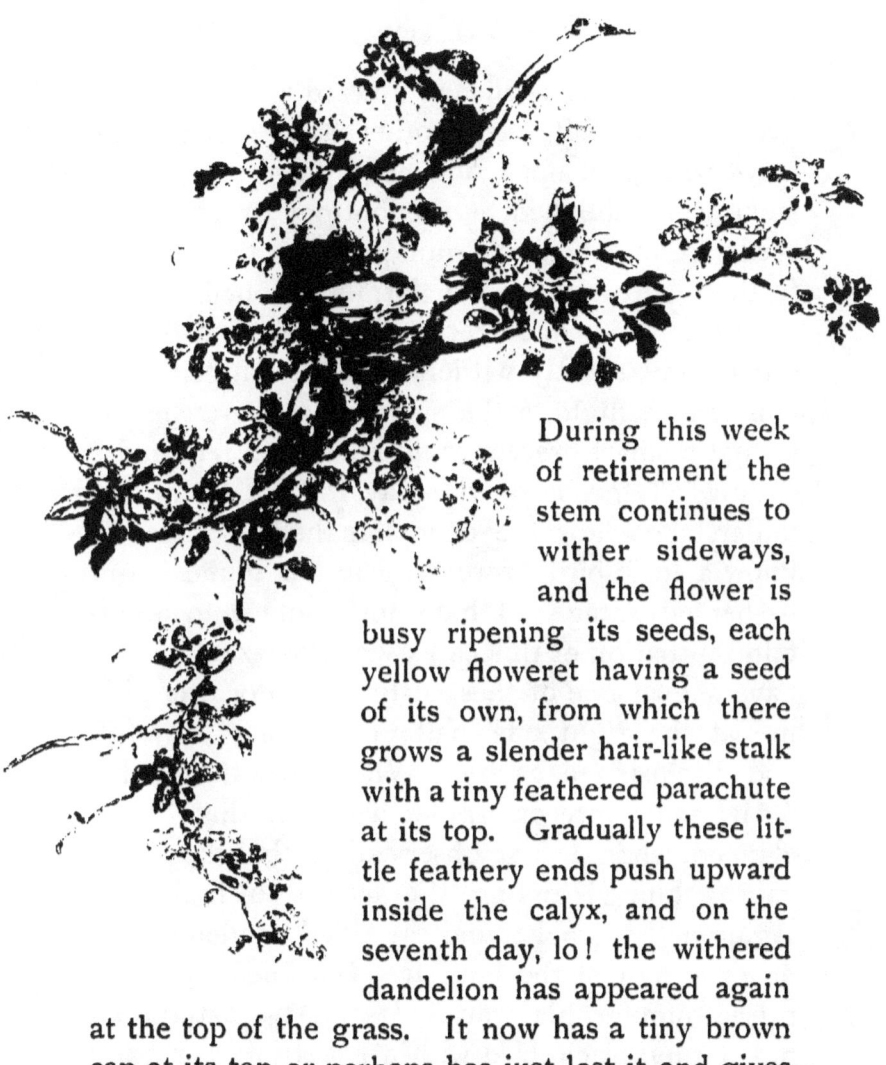

During this week of retirement the stem continues to wither sideways, and the flower is busy ripening its seeds, each yellow floweret having a seed of its own, from which there grows a slender hair-like stalk with a tiny feathered parachute at its top. Gradually these little feathery ends push upward inside the calyx, and on the seventh day, lo! the withered dandelion has appeared again at the top of the grass. It now has a tiny brown cap at its top, or perhaps has just lost it, and gives us a glimpse of a white feathery tuft peeping from its top. This little brown withered cap is all that is left of the original golden blossom of two weeks before, now a shrivelled mass, which has gradually been pushed upward and out by the growing seed-tuft. In another hour, perhaps, the calyx will again open, and bend down against the stem, while the bed at the bottom to which the seeds are attached will round upward through the feathers outward in the form of a ball. This rounded seed-bed, or receptacle, as it is called in our botany, shortly withers, and the winged parachutes take flight at the slightest zephyr, whereas at first a smart breeze would have been required.

Now all this is by-the-way, for not every one understands how the dandelion ball is made. I know a little bird, however, who has found it out to her advantage. I have just alluded to a certain mutilation of this calyx which puzzled me. I have shown one of these calyxes in my title picture, at the right, one-half of it being torn off, and disclosing a cavity. Where are the seeds? "Ah! some rare caterpillar has done this!" I exclaimed, when I first observed the burglary. In vain I hunted among the leaves to find him. Again and again I found my rifled dandelion, but never a sign of the burglar. But one day I surprised him at his work. It was no caterpillar, but a tiny, black bird with a beautiful rosy band in his tail, and which proved to be that butterfly among the birds, the redstart. I hardly knew what he was doing out there among the dandelions, and presumed he was after my mysterious caterpillar, until I chanced to see him alight near by with a white tuft in his bill. Yes, a tuft with feathery parachutes in a bunch on one side of his bill, and a compact cluster of seeds on the other.

In a moment I was among the dandelions from which he had flown, and soon found my empty calyx, from which an entire dandelion ball had been taken at one pinch. I lost no time in tracing out the nest in the foot of an apple-tree close by. A dainty fabric it was, exquisitely adorned with gray lichens and skeletonized leaves, its interior very plentifully lined with the seeds of the dandelion, more so than is usual with the nests of this bird. On two occasions since I have seen other small birds of the warbler kind suspiciously rummaging among the dandelions, and have afterwards discovered the empty calyx. There is probably more than one dandelion burglar.

The Troubles of the House-fly

QUITE contrary to my original intention, my specimen of *Musca domestica*, which I had captured at random to serve as my model in the present chapter, has suggested that I begin with a Q, and after some expressive criticism on the matter I have at last consented to humor him, especially as he proved otherwise a most unique and accommodating individual. Being in need of a good, healthy, toe-twisting, neck-twirling specimen to sit for his portrait in an illustration for a forthcoming article on the paper wasp, I cast my eye about my easel. There, right at my elbow, still plying his never-ending toilet, I beheld him— strange coincidence, was it not? A sweep of my hand, and I have him! And in a moment more, with the tips of his toes besmeared with glue, he is a secure prisoner on the white paper before me.

The victim having served his purpose, I was preparing to drench him with a few drops of water to dissolve his bonds and set him free, when I happened to observe a feature which had before escaped my notice. The glue had chanced to secure one of its feet well beneath its body, and now that it was released I discovered that I had made considerably more of a catch with that sweep of my hand than I had imagined. Attached to one of the terminal joints of the front leg there appeared a tiny red object, which I instantly recognized as a curious tag which I had seen before, and which forms an occasional lively episode in the life not only of house-flies but other flies as well. And what a queer-shaped tag it is, to be sure! It is not easy to describe its dimensions on account of its changeable proportions—now spreading out its two long appendages, now contracting into an oblong or rounded outline, or sprawled out in the shape of a curious letter T, and now thrown about in such a helter-skelter fashion by the antics of the fly that nothing but the fact of its red color is discernible. But when we bring our magnifying-glass to bear upon it, its diminutive size is forgotten, while its shape is now perfectly familiar to us all—a lobster! a veritable live young lobster, and what is even more strange, a live boiled lobster at that! No, it must be a crab lobster, for was ever the liveliest lobster in its greenest stages half so spry as this warlike midge, whose free, upraised, open claws threaten to nip our fingers off as we hold the lens above him. But nag and prod him as we will, no provocation will induce him to loosen his grip on his means of transport.

For how many days, I wonder, has he been on this particular flying trip? How many miles has he travelled, and what varied experiences has he survived! How many are the lumps of sugar, the drops of molasses, the slices of bread, and pats of butter over which he has been trailed, to say nothing of puddles of fresh ink! And then think of the many hours in which, from his present position, he must have conspicuously figured at that toe-twisting toilet of his host! Fancy brushing your coat and combing your hair with a live boiled lobster!

But pollen grains are not pumpkins and footballs and tea-boxes, as the microscope would have us believe; nor does the drop of water contain a herd of strange elephants. Can it be possible that this lobster is, after all, only about an eighth of an inch long, with its claws spreading barely three-sixteenths of an inch? Yes, true; but we must remember that the fly is only about one-third of an inch long, and we can imagine how proportionately formidable the little beast must appear as a lurking foe and a handicap to the fly fraternity. I have therefore pictured this little episode of fly-time somewhat from the aspect of the fly. This was one of the "troubles" which I had in mind as I prepared the initial design with its letter O. I had counted on using an old specimen of the lobster which I had safely stowed away in a pill-box somewhere, until my haphazard fly victim supplied me with a fresh specimen, and subsequently helped me out in the completion and modification of my initial.

A correct idea of the anatomy of the little crab may be obtained from my illustration. But what is it all about, this funny ride on a fly's hind-leg? Excepting as an inconvenience and encumbrance it is doubtful whether the fly is much the worse for his close attachment, and while this mimic crab or lobster cannot be called a frequent passenger, a careful scrutiny of any considerable assemblage of flies on white paper or window-pane will occasionally show us the animated and persistent red tag.

But let us call him a lobster no more, rather one of the " False Scorpions," one of the group

known as *Pedipalpi*, in the books: queer little creatures that live in dusty nooks, among old books and papers, and feed on tiny mites and other minute life which harbor them, but born rovers withal, with a singular fancy for fly-toes and free rides.

But the false scorpion may be considered rather as a bother than a serious trouble to the fly. His real troubles are too numerous to mention. His life, as most of my readers will be glad to learn, is not a bed of roses, as is commonly supposed. Just think for a moment what a fly's existence must be. With the deadly fly-paper on the one hand, the continual danger of being cemented into a pellet of pulp in the maw of a hornet, or impaled on the beak of his murderous relative the "Laphria-fly," or snapped up by birds, toads, snakes, he certainly has abundant use for that head full of eyes of his. All summer long he runs the gantlet of risks like these, but in September and October a new and terrible danger awaits him, and fortunate is he if he escapes in these advanced days of scientific discovery, when so many of our mortal ills are shown to be dependent upon the malignity of hovering germs, of microbes, bacteria, and bacilli.

Let us be thankful we have at least escaped the notice of one of this insidious throng, and are spared the grotesque horror of such a fate as the germ-scourge of flydom. How swift and terrible is its course! To-day a pert and gladsome innocent, sipping on the rim of our dinner-plate; to-morrow a pale, dry relic of his former self, hanging from the window-pane by its tongue, and enveloped in a white shroud of mould, the victim of a germ or spore. Look where we will upon the window on those September and October days and we see the little smoky cloud with the dangling fly in its midst, and many an apparently modest and considerate fly upon the wall will be found similarly fixed to the surface, and surrounded with the white nimbus.

But the real mischief was done perhaps early in the evening, after our fly had retired for the night. He presumably experienced the first attack of acute dyspepsia he had ever known. In his promiscuous feeding he had chanced to imbibe a spore, which once within his vitals began its murderous work, growing so fast as to completely fill his swelling body by morning, when, having completed its growth and penetrated through the insect's skin, it spread its own spores, to be wafted hither and yon to the peril of next year's flies, and the consequent delight of the tidy house-keeper.

Such is the work of the world-renowned fly-fungus, of which a writer says: " It silences more house-flies than all the brushes, traps, poisons, whacks, and swearing devoted to the extermination of the insect."

Tendrils

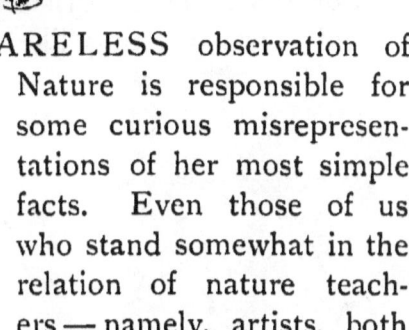

CARELESS observation of Nature is responsible for some curious misrepresentations of her most simple facts. Even those of us who stand somewhat in the relation of nature teachers — namely, artists, both draughtsmen and painters, and from whom we have a right to expect absolute fidelity — are not free from our shortcomings as truthful chroniclers. Thus how often we see otherwise beautiful landscapes marred by features which rebel against all laws of natural philosophy — of a storm sky above a sunlit scene, for instance, spanned by the arc of the rainbow, and with all the shadows of trees and other objects thrown sidewise! Then there is that inverted or very "dry" crescent moon in western twilight skies; and how seldom do we see the beautiful law of the twining tendril appreciated in the most careful design of the botanical draughtsman!

For years the tendril was to me the conventional spiral, twisting like a continuous curl or spring from the parent branch to the support within its clasp; and it is safe to assert that not one in—well, a good many of us, who should have gone out to our grape-vine or passion-vine or melon-patch, without a previous forewarning, would have been able to tell correctly the pretty little story of its tendril methods, or have even noted the curious little kink which is the infallible peculiarity of the climbing tendril.

What *is* a tendril—botanically speaking? That depends. It is one thing in this plant, quite another in that, so students of vegetable anatomy or morphology soon discover.

It is soon perfectly plain that the stem is a modified root. For instance, plants have been taken up from the sod and replaced in the ground upsidedown, the roots subsequently becoming stems, and bearing leaves, and the buried leafy stems assuming the functions of roots. Leaves are mere modified branches, and the flowers modified leaves. Pistils and stamens in flowers are modified petals, or rather petals are modified stamens, the "doubling" of flowers representing the being thus accomplished, while the petals again are mere changed leaves. A neighbor of mine has a bush bearing green roses—all leaves. In the water-lily you will find it difficult to determine just where the stamen ends and the petals begin, so gradual is the blending. In the peony the same is true, and carried still further in the merging of petals and calyx into the approximate leaves.

And so it is with tendrils. In certain plants the point of the leaf, through ages of "natural selection," has gradually been prolonged into a slender arm, which clasps the branches of trees, and enables the plant thus endowed to climb higher to sun and sky, and thus to thrive more vigorously than its less fortunate brothers. The plant so advantageously equipped transmits its tendency to its offspring, and has therefore survived in place of its ancient fellows, and is the type perpetuated or "selected" by nature. Such a tendril, then, is a modified leaf. How is it in the pea? Here we find four leaflets in two opposite pairs, but *no odd leaflet* at the end of the main stalk, such as we see in almost all other plants of its family. But in place of this leaflet we find a branch-

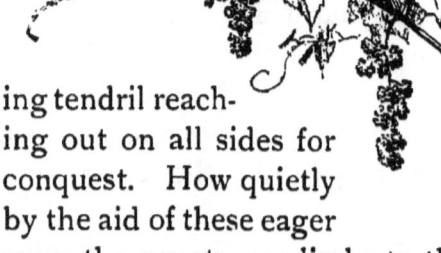

ing tendril reaching out on all sides for conquest. How quietly by the aid of these eager arms the sweet-pea climbs to the top of its brush! In the common catbrier or smilax we see two slender thread-like tendrils growing from the base of each leaf. Here we have another modification, a development of the "stipule," that tiny pointed growth common to many leaves, and particularly notable at the base of a rose leaf. Still another plan has been evolved in the grape-vine. If we examine our grape arbor in June we find a number of drooping, swaying branches. The leaves are scattered singly at intervals of a few inches along the branch, each of the upper ones being attended on its opposite side by a drooping cluster of mignonette-scented blossoms. Thus they follow down towards the tip of the branch, where the clusters suddenly cease, and are replaced by long, slender, curving and branched tendrils, sometimes ten inches long. We might thus reasonably assume the tendril in this case to be a modified blossom cluster, but there is no need for us ever to assume such a thing. If we will only search with sufficient care we shall at last discover the absolute proof of the fact in a tendril which is partly in blossom, the nearest leaf-joint above it having a full cluster of blossoms, and the tendril below it, nearer the tip, not a few scattered flower-buds at its tips. This grape-vine instance may be taken as a demonstration that in no case is the tendril a special or primal organ, but merely an old one adapted to a new purpose. In one instance from a leaf, in another from a flower-stalk, just which can generally be determined by a sufficient search for the telltale *intermediate form* somewhere to be found on the plant.

Among the most beautiful of all tendrils are those of the passion-flower and plants of the melon family, notably the wild star-cucumber,

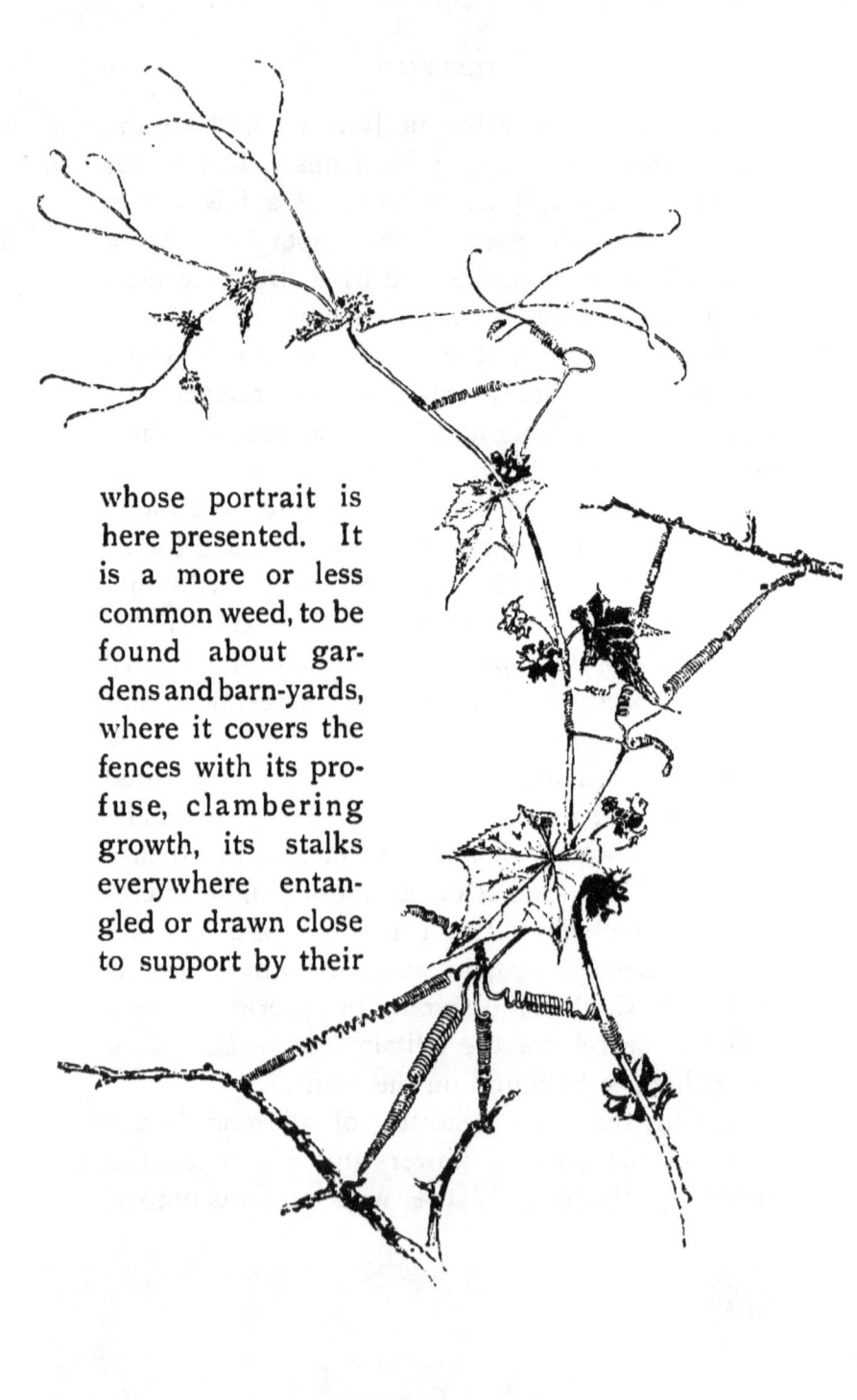

whose portrait is here presented. It is a more or less common weed, to be found about gardens and barn-yards, where it covers the fences with its profuse, clambering growth, its stalks everywhere entangled or drawn close to support by their long, green, spiral springs, and its free, branching, young tendril tips reaching out in all directions for fresh foothold, and in its absence content at length with a friendly intertwining among themselves, and a consequent tangle of green convolutions. It is hard to believe that these long, outreaching arms at the summit of this vine are identical with the closely twisted spirals below, but such is the case; let any one of them once feel the contact of even the frailest support of twig or stalk, and it is soon close in the embrace of its eager tip, and the contraction of the spring commences, but the method of this contraction is worth our study.

In order for this tendril to coil it must *twist*, and it is perfectly plain on general principles that with both ends held fast twisting is impossible. But this little paradox is evidently dismissed by the tendril. If we tie a short string between two given points, and attempt to twist it with our finger and thumb, we succeed in turning the string, 'tis true, but the twist on the right side neutralizes that on the left, being in the opposite direction. In this way only can the cord be twisted. If we twist with sufficient patience we may imitate the coil of the tendril, which is performed precisely in this way. Herein lies the secret of that little loop or kink in the centre of all tendrils—a given point, which cannot be determined on the extended tendril, but whose mission is to *reverse* the twist in opposite directions as soon as the tip has secured its contact, and thus permit the coiling process to proceed. In tendrils of exceeding length several of these reverse loops may be found at regular intervals, sometimes as many as six in a single tendril, but the coiling process usually awaits this contact. Unsatisfied tendrils of the grape, for instance, will remain unchanged through the entire season, or until their sensitive touch has been lost. Others, like those of the passion-flower, will occasionally become discouraged and curl up all by themselves, in which case, the other tip being free, the curl is perfect and continuous and without the reverse loop, which is now unnecessary. But the function of the tendril is to clasp and hold. Its growth is not complete until thus quickened by the new responsibility. Tendrils on duty become tough and sinewy in comparison to their idling neighbors. How firm and rigid are these swollen coils upon the grape-vine!

We do not gather "figs from thistles," but some equally incongruous botanical associates are sometimes brought about through the insinuating and clambering methods of the tendril. Have we not all seen apple-trees bearing pumpkins or squashes or gourds, all originally carried thither in the form of great yellow blossoms or tender shoots! The grape-vine occasionally plays a singular botanical prank in the orchard. Here is a drooping tendril which has been swinging about for weeks from its vine canopy on the old apple-tree. It had become almost discouraged, when a chance-favoring breeze wafted its tip in contact with an apple close by. It was its last chance; with its hooked extremity it clasped the stem of the fruit, and soon made itself fast with three or four firm coils. Doubtless the little reversing loop somewhere along the tendril was also awakened from its chronic lethargy, and did its best to start the coil. Presumably it succeeded, for the pull was sufficient to dislodge the apple, which, falling to the entire length of the tendril, was still held fast in the grip, whose new responsibility had given it new strength.

And there our apple hung for weeks, swinging like a pendulum from the slender grape-vine, the coils on duty still keeping their firm grip on the stem, even though all above were straightened by the weight of the burden.

A Strange Story of a Grasshopper

A FEW days ago, while returning from a walk, I chanced to observe a dead grasshopper upon the dirt at the side of the road. Now this incident would not have been of special importance had I not discovered, upon careful *post-mortem* examination, the very remarkable manner of the insect's death, which recalled a similar surprising episode of several years ago which I had almost forgotten. Upon referring to my note-book of that period, however, I found considerable space devoted to the incident, which greatly astonished me at the time. Inasmuch as it presents in a startling light the wonderful and strange resources by which nature holds in check the too rapid increase of species and maintains the great law of equilibrium among the insect forces, it is well worth recalling in these pages, in the firm belief that my young entomological readers will henceforth look more compassionately and tenderly upon the poor "high-elbowed grig" who is the unfortunate hero of my story. He is familiar to us all, that hovering "rattler" above the hot, dusty road of August, flying up from nowhere beneath our feet in the path, fluttering like a yellow moth, and always disappearing before our eyes when he alights. He is also known as the "Quaker," from his drab suit and bonnet, and his generosity with his "molasses" is proverbial from the days of the Pilgrim settlers. Who would have believed that such a fate as the following lay in store for him.

In previous papers I have indicated some of the remarkable pranks which the various ichneumon-flies play with unsuspecting caterpillars. The polyphemus, for instance, whose cocoon, filled with hopes of a beautiful butterfly existence, yields only a swarm of wasps. The caterpillars are helpless, and would seem an easy prey to the wily fly who lays her eggs upon them; but even the agile-winged "Quaker," and doubtless many of his kind—yes, and still more agile insects—are not quick enough to escape a like fate.

At the time of my discovery I had in preparation an article for "Harper's Magazine" entitled "Among Our Footprints." I wished to describe and illustrate a singular battle which I had shortly before observed between a large red mutilla ant and a "Quaker." The mutilla I had captured at the time, and had preserved as a specimen. I needed only the grasshopper to complete my drawing. Directly in front of my city house a

number of vacant grassy lots offered a favorite haunt for the insects — I used to call it the Quaker camp-meeting ground—and I started out to procure one. Having no net, I was soon convinced that I was greatly at a disadvantage. The thermometer was about 90°, and, of course, the "Quakers," being in their element, had much the best, not to say the easiest, time of it. I at length gave up the chase, and was about leaving the field, when fortune favored me by the discovery of a clumsy specimen, which seemed unable to fly for any great length, and he was soon captured. Upon examination his wings seemed partially paralyzed, but otherwise he appeared to be in good health and spirits, his hind legs being especially lively and snappy. I immediately took the insect to my studio, and pinned him through the thorax. He was strong enough to pull out the pin from the board and jump around the room with it in my temporary absence.

I lost no time in taking his portrait, which figured in the illustration to the article on "Footprints" as "the ungainly victim," I little dreaming when I gave him such a title what a remarkable sort of victim he even then was. The drawing took me about ten minutes. I then left the studio, and was absent precisely fifteen minutes. Upon returning I found the grasshopper dead.

My curiosity was aroused, not only by such a rapid demise (for the impaling through the thorax is not usually an immediately fatal injury to an insect), but especially by some very strange and unnatural automatic movements of the victim—head protruding and turning from side to side; queer expansion of body, as though breathing; unusual lifting and other motions of legs, particularly of hind legs; the whole demonstration a mockery on life. The grasshopper was pinned to my drawing-board, and against a piece of newspaper. As I watched his strange antics, I suddenly discovered that he had become a veritable phantom of his former self; that I could actually *read the newspaper text through his body.* Examination now revealed the mystery. I could easily see every nook and cranny of the grasshopper's interior, so glassy were the walls of the body, and I could now count about a dozen small, white larvæ, which were now full grown, and were crawling about within through head, thorax, body, and hind legs, cleaning its walls of every particle of remaining tissue, and causing the singular motions described. Such a strange house-cleaning I never saw before.

When the "Quaker" locust was captured it showed not the slightest sign of any such goings-on within its being. The final voracity of the larvæ was swift and terrible. And what an astonishing instinct is that which should teach these parasites to avoid the vitals of their insect host until the last moments of their own final, complete growth! The entire space of time from the activity of the grasshopper to the empty, transparent phantom was less than thirty minutes. I placed the unfortunate victim in a small, close box. Next morning he presented nothing but a clean, glassy shell, now more glassy than before, empty of every vestige of organic matter, while scattered about on the bottom of the box lay fifteen dark red, egg-shaped chrysalides of the escaped larvæ. Two weeks later, upon opening the box, a swarm of flies flew out. I was enabled to keep two of them. They were almost exactly like the common house-fly to the ordinary ob-

server, but belonged to a distinct genus. At this writing, in the absence of my specimen, I cannot give the name by which they are known in learned circles, but I think I am safe in saying that they probably belong to the group called *Tachina*, a family of parasitic flies which spend their early lives in a similar questionable manner, to the probable discomfort of potato-bugs, caterpillars, and other accommodating insect hosts.

I had seen similar flies emerging from my caterpillar boxes in my early entomological days without suspecting their significance, and any large collection of caterpillars in confinement is likely to include a victim.

Riddles in Flowers

INDEED, are they not all riddles? Where is the flower which even to the most devoted of us has yet confided all its mysteries? In comparison with the insight of the earlier botanists, we have surely come much closer to the flowers, and they have imparted many of their secrets to us. Through the inspired vision of Sprengel, Darwin, and their followers we have learned something of their meaning, in addition to the knowledge of their structure, which comprised the end and aim of the study of those early scholars, Linnæus, Lindley, Jussieu, and De Candolle. To these and other eminent worthies in botany we owe much of our knowledge of *how* the flowers are made, and of the classification based upon this structure, but if these great savants had been asked, "You have shown us that it *is so*, but *why* is it thus?" they could only have replied, "We know not; we only know that an all-wise Providence has so ordained and created it."

Take this little collection, which I have here presented, of stamens and petals selected at random from common blossoms. What inexplicable riddles to the botanist of a hundred years ago, even of sixty years ago! For not until that time

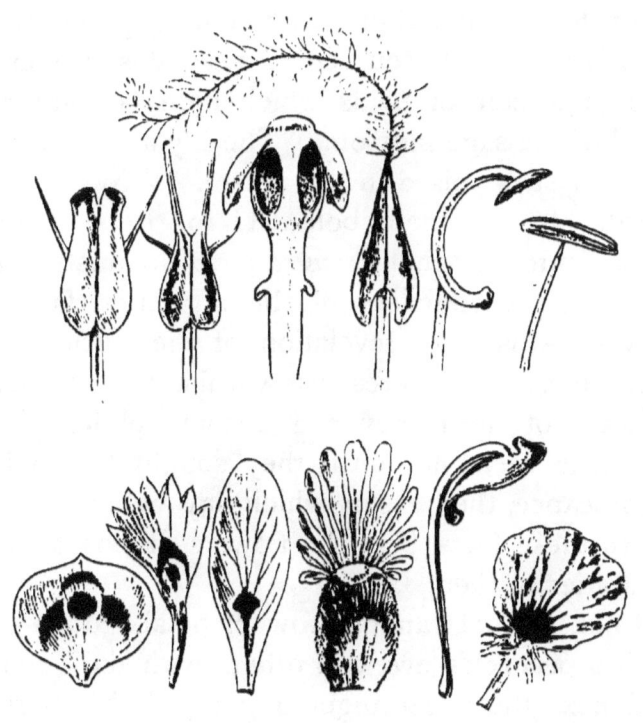

was their significance fully understood; and yet each of these presents but one of several equally puzzling features in the same flowers from which they were taken.

In that first anther, for example, why those pores at the tip of the cells, instead of the usual slits at the sides, and why that pair of horns at the back? And the next one, with longer tubes, and the same two horns besides! Then there is that queer specimen with flapping ears—one of six from the barberry blossom; and the pointed, arrow-headed individual with a long plume from its apex; and the curved C-shaped specimen— one of a pair of twins which hide beneath the hood of the sage blossom. The lily anther, which comes last, is poised in the centre. Why? What puzzles to the mere botanist! for it is because these eminent scholars *were mere* botanists—students and chroniclers of the structural facts of flowers—that this revelation of the truth about these blossom features was withheld from them. It was not until they had become philosophers and true seers, not until they sought the divine significance, the reason, which lay behind or beneath these facts, that the flowers disclosed their mysteries to them.

Look at that random row of petals, too!—one with a peacock's eye, two others with dark spots, and next the queer-fingered petal of the mignonette, followed by one of that queer couple of the monk's-hood blossom which no one ever sees unless he tears the flower hood to pieces. We all know the nasturtium, but have we thought to ask it why these petals have such a deep crimson or orange colored spot, and why each one is so beautifully fringed at the edge of its stalk?

These are but a dozen of the millions of similar challenges, riddles, puzzles, which the commonest flowers of field and garden present to us; and yet we claim to "know" our nasturtium, our pink, our monk's-hood larkspur, our daisy, and violet!

No; we must be *more* than "botanists" before we can hope to understand the flowers, with their endless, infinite variety of form, color, and fragrance.

It was not until the flowers were studied in connection with the insects which visit them that the true secret of these puzzling features became suspected.

We all know, or should know, that the anther in flowers secretes and releases the pollen. For years even the utility of this pollen was a mystery. Not until the year 1682 was its purpose guessed, when Nehemias Grew, an English botanist, discovered that unless its grains reached the stigma in the flower no seed would be produced (Diagram A). But the people refused to believe this, and it was not until fifty years later that Grew's statement was fully accepted, and then only because the great Linnæus assured the world that it *was* true. But about fifty years later another botanist in Germany, Sprengel, made the discovery that the flower could not be fertilized as these botanists had claimed, that

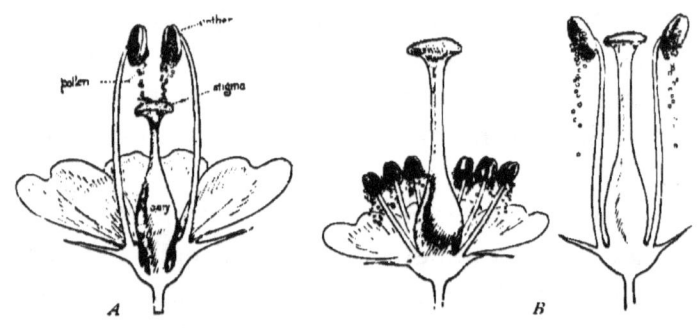

in many blossoms the pollen could not fall on the stigma.

Sprengel knew that this pollen must reach the stigma, but showed that in most flowers it could not do so by *itself*. He saw that insects were always working in the flowers, and that their hairy bodies were generally covered with pollen, and in this way pollen grains *were* continually carried to the stigma, as they could easily be in these two blossoms shown at Diagram B. Sprengel then announced to the world his theory — the dawn of discovery, the beginning of the solution of all these floral riddles. The *insect* explained it all. The bright colors and fragrance were intended to attract him, and the nectar to reward him, and while thus sipping he conveyed the pollen to the stigma and fertilized the flower.

But now Sprengel himself was met with most discouraging opposition to his theory, showing that he had guessed but half the secret after all. Flowers by the hundreds were brought to his notice, like that shown in Diagram C, in which

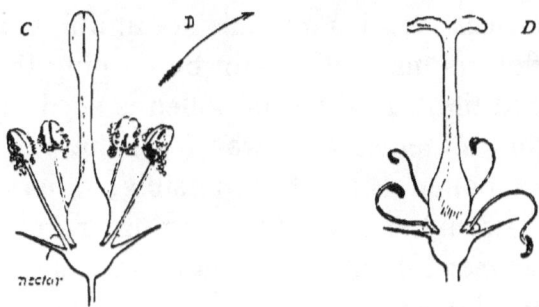

the insect could *not* transfer the pollen from anther to stigma, as the stigma is closed when the pollen is ripe, and like that in Diagram D, which does not open until the pollen is shed. For seventy years this astonishing fact puzzled the world, and was at last solved by the great Darwin, who showed that nearly all flowers shun their own pollen, and are so constructed, by thousands of singular devices, that the *insect* shall bring to each the *pollen of another flower* of the same species, and thus effect what is known as *cross-fertilization*.

We must then look at all flowers as expressions of welcome to some insect—day-flowering blossoms mostly to bees and butterflies, and night-bloomers to moths. And not only expressions of welcome, but each with some perfect little plan of its own to make this insect guest the bearer of its pollen to the stigma of another flower of the same species. And how endless are the plans and devices to insure this beautiful scheme! Some flowers make it certain by keeping the stigma closed tight until all its pollen is shed; others place the anther so far away from the stigma as to make pollen contact impossible; others actually imprison these pollen-bringing insects until they can send them away with fresh pollen all over their bodies.

Take almost any flower we chance to meet, and it will show us a mystery of form which the insect alone can explain.

Here is one, growing just outside my door—a blossom "known" even to every child, and certainly to every reader of the "Round Table"—the pretty bluets, or Houstonia, whose galaxy of white or blue stars tints whole spring meadows like a light snowfall. We have "known" it all our lives. Perhaps we may have chanced to observe that the flowers are not all constructed alike, but the chances are that we have *seen* them *all our lives* without discovering this fact. If we pluck a few from this dense cluster beside the path, we observe that the throat of each is swollen larger than the tube beneath, and is almost closed by four tiny yellow anthers (Fig. 1). The next and the next clump may show us similar flowers; but after a little search we are sure of finding a cluster in which a new form appears, as shown in Fig. 2, in which the anthers at the opening are missing, and their place supplied with a little forked stigma! The tube below is larger than the first flower for about two-thirds its length, when it suddenly contracts, and if we cut it open we find the four anthers secreted near the wide base of the tube. What does it mean, this riddle of the bluets? For hundreds of years it puzzled the early botanists, only finally to be solved by Darwin. This is simply the little plan which the Houstonia has perfected to insure its cross-fertilization by an insect, to compel an insect to carry its pollen from one flower and deposit it upon the stigma of another. Once realizing this as the secret, we can readily see how perfectly the intention is fulfilled.

In order to make it clear I have drawn a progressive series of pictures which hardly require

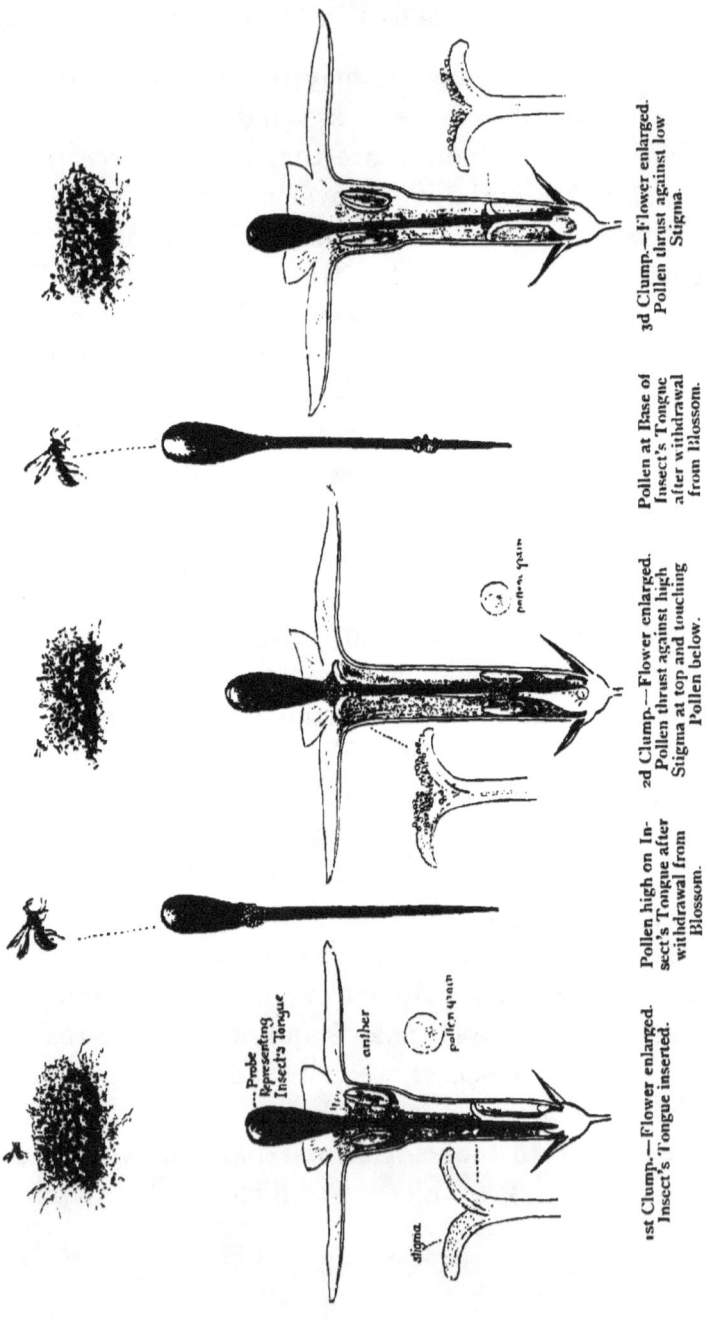

description. The flowers are visited by small bees, butterflies, and other insects. At the left is an insect just alighting on a clump of the blossoms of the high-anther form indicated below it. The black probe represents the insect's tongue, which, as it seeks the nectar at the bottom of the tube, gets dusted at its thickened top with the pollen from the anthers. We next see the insect flying away, the probe beneath indicating the condition of its tongue. It next alights on clump No. 2, in which the flowers happen to be of the high-stigma form, as shown below. The tongue now being inserted, brings the pollen against the high stigma, and fertilizes the flower, while at the same time its tip comes in contact with the low anthers, and gets pollen from them. We next see the insect flying to clump No. 3, the condition of its tongue being shown below. Clump No. 3 happens to be of the first low-stigma form of flowers, and as the tongue is inserted the pollen at its tip is carried directly to the low stigma, and *this* flower is fertilized from the pollen from the anthers on the same level in the previous flower. And thus the riddle is solved by the insect. From clump to clump he flies, and through his help each one of the pale blue blooms is sure to get its food, each flower fertilized by the pollen of another.

Another beautiful provision is seen in the difference in size of the pollen-grain of the two flowers, those of the high anthers being much larger than those from the lower anthers. These larger grains are intended for the high stigma, which they are sure of reaching, while those of smaller size, on the top of the tongue, which should happen to be wiped off on the high stigma, are too small to be effective for fertilization.

Luck in Clovers

UNDER one guise or another the fickle goddess Fortuna would seem to have established her infallible interpreters or mediators. The lovelorn maiden with the daisy, its petals falling beneath her questioning finger-tips to the alternate refrain, "He loves me. He loves me not," is a sacrificial episode in the life of the daisy wherever it grows.

The still younger maiden with her dandelion ball, whose feathered parachutes must be dislodged upon the breeze with three puffs from her little puckered mouth, with all sorts of fate depending upon the odd or even number of the remnant seeds, is as universal as the dandelion itself, while the more homely symbols of wish-bone, horseshoe, or horse-chestnut, as we all know, are proverbially potent as personal or household charms against ill luck. I once knew a shrewd countryman who gave all the credit of his success in "tradin'" to the "hoss-chestnut" which he carried in his pocket, and would as soon think of throwing his money away as to "drive a trade" without it. More than one old "down-East" dame "sets gre't store" by the horseshoe hung above her doorway, always secured ends up, "so's the luck can't run out." Then there was old Aunt Huldy, who, while she claimed to locate springs and wells the country round by her witch-hazel divining-rod, never ventured upon these expeditions without the concealed necklace of dried star puff-balls hung about her neck.

But perhaps the most universal of all these natural symbols of good-fortune is to be found in the four-leaved clover, almost a world-wide superstition, and traced back to the ancient astrologers. "If a man, walking the fields," writes one of them, "finds any four-leaved grasse, he shall in a short while after finde some good thing."

The clover was considered as being especially "noisome to witches," and the "holy trefoil charm" was a powerful spell against their harm; the "trefoil" being the most widely used title of the clover—*Trifolium*, as it is in the botany—three leaved. And such it *should* be, to be true to its christening. But it frequently takes exception to the botany and gives us an extra leaf, and thus we have our "four-leaved clover," a rarity which many of us, seek as we will, have never yet been able to discover in its native haunt, even though a whole handful of them are plucked here and there before our eyes by our more favored companions. Indeed, there are some lucky folk who seem literally to stumble upon "four-leaved grasse" wherever they go—who, having found one leaf, will sit down quietly in the grass and ere long accumulate a bouquet.

Yes, here's the secret: It is not your eager gadding quest that gets your four-leaved clover. Nor is it all a matter of "sharp eyes." There is a "knack" about finding four-leaved clover, and this very knack of the so-called "lucky ones," implying as it does the operation of quest, observation, and common-sense, would logically argue a corresponding fulfilment of success in the affairs of daily life. For the observant clover-hunter, if his mind and eye work together, soon learns that the "four-leaved" variety is fond of company, and that the whim of the plant which thus produces one such leaf is very apt to be humored in several others. Thus, having discerned *one* four-leaved clover, we assume a *tendency* in the parent plant, which further search often discloses, sometimes to our great surprise, and, if we are as superstitious as our antique philosopher above quoted, to our unbounded satisfaction. If, for instance, this one extra leaflet brings such assurance of "good things" to come, what shall be said of a leaf with five or six leaflets—yes, seven, or perhaps eight—I might even add nine—a veritable little green rose of clover leaves, all on one stem, a stem which is sometimes plainly composite, of two or three adherent stems? All of these exuberant forms are to be found with diligent search, and often in the same close vicinity. Nor are these all the varied freaks which the plant will disclose for the seeking. Perhaps you may chance upon that four-leaved variety in which the extra leaflet stands upright in the midst of the three, and is transformed into a tapering cup. These elfin goblets are not exceedingly rare. Occasionally we may chance to find two of these supported by one or two perfect leaflets at the base. Or, if we are especially fortunate, our "good health" may be offered in three of the tiny beakers, not mere *apparent* cups, but with the edges of the goblets completely united, and which might be filled to the brim with dew.

A collection of the natural whims of the clover, both red and white, would make an interesting leaflet in our herbarium. In the hands of the floriculturist who should cultivate these eccentricities most remarkable varieties of clover might

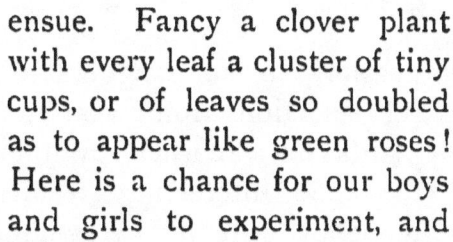

ensue. Fancy a clover plant with every leaf a cluster of tiny cups, or of leaves so doubled as to appear like green roses! Here is a chance for our boys and girls to experiment, and

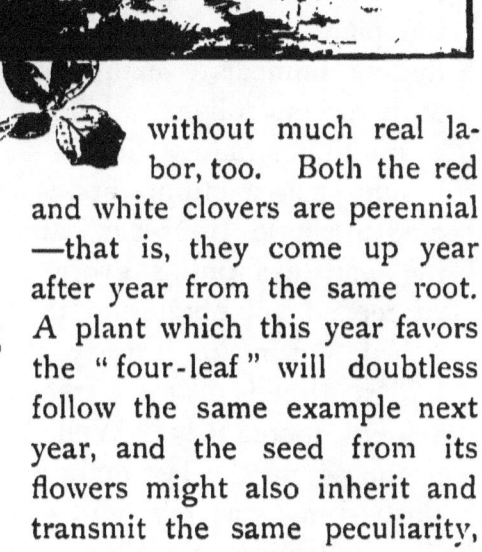

without much real labor, too. Both the red and white clovers are perennial—that is, they come up year after year from the same root. A plant which this year favors the "four-leaf" will doubtless follow the same example next year, and the seed from its flowers might also inherit and transmit the same peculiarity, possibly in an exaggerated degree; and careful selection from year to year, keeping the plants in a corner by themselves, might lead to some interesting results, especially if the tendency were further stimulated by enrichment of soil, to which the clover responds vigorously.

My experience with "clover luck" has been considerable. I believe I have found almost every possible eccentric combination of which the plant is naturally capable, a few of which I have here pictured.

My best success has been met in the "rowen" fields, or the growth after mowing, the energy of the plant, thus pruned as it were in its prime, finding immediate expression in an exuberance of luxuriant foliage, which, I think, inclines to a multiplication of leaves. I once sat down beside such a clump upon which I had discovered a single "four-leaf," and by dint of plucking and examining every leaf in the cluster, succeeded in obtaining thirty-nine specimens. "Why not make it forty while you are about it?" a friend of mine recently remarked, with evident incredulity. Well, I *tried* to, but after grubbing up the last embryo leaf at the ground, thirty-nine was my limit — all from one plant. The collection might be subdivided as follows: Four leaves, 22; five leaves, 7; six leaves, 3;

seven leaves, 1 ; nine leaves, 1 ; cups and leaves, various, 5.

At another time I spied a single five-leaved in a dense bed of rowen clover at the road-side, and seating myself close beside it, calculating on this habit of the plant, I vowed I would not get up until I had collected forty multiple leaves. I soon obtained more than this number.

The clover-leaf quest is a good eye-sharpener. Which of our boys can show us the best record?

I wonder if any of my young readers have ever seen how the clover says its prayers and goes to sleep, with its two side leaflets folded together like reverent palms, and the terminal leaflet bowed above them? So the normal leaf spends the night in the dews. I often wonder what arrangement of adjustment is arrived at when so many leaflets conspire to confuse.

My clover-hunting has been confined to the red and white clovers, both species having common tendencies. In the red, the leaves being larger, the freaks are more conspicuous, but the cup forms seem more commonly identified with the white clover.

Barberry Manners

ONE who is unfamiliar with the remarkable doings of blossoms in association with their insect honey-sippers might consider it somewhat surprising to attribute "manners" to a flower. But who that has seen the sage-blossom clap its bee visitor on the back as she ushers him in at the threshold of her purple door, marking him for her own with her dab of yellow pollen as she almost pushes him into the nectar feast within; who that has witnessed the almost roguish demonstration which the tiny andromeda-bell extends to the sipping bee at its doorway—who that has seen these can any longer doubt that blossoms have "manners" as well as we bigger, more con-

scious beings? Yes, manners, unquestionably—
"bad manners," it would almost seem, in some instances, as, for example, in this andromeda blossom-bell, which, in its perfume and its nectar, deliberately invites the tiny *Andrena* bee, only to deluge its little, black, hairy face with a smothering shower of dusty pollen. A remarkable style of etiquette, surely, that is, from our *human* standpoint. But in the realm of Flora the standards of decorum, so far as greeting is concerned, are not governed by artificial whim. There is no "smart set" to dictate and set the fashion for others less smart to follow. Each individual flower is a law unto itself as to the method of its greeting to its especial insect friend. The blossom etiquette of welcome is literally as "old as the hills," and has come down with little change from an ancestry which dates back perhaps to a period when there were no human "ancestors" on the globe. So these "manners" are natural and original, to say the least, even if they are so queer sometimes. What would you think of a friend whose hospitable smile and welcome at his doorway should invite you thither only that your foot might touch a trigger and let fall the floor beneath you, while at the same time you are half suffocated with an explosion of a bushel of yellow corn meal? Yet such is something like the spectacular reception which the lotus clover, the des-

modium, and the genista flowers consider the most expressive form of welcome. But the little bees seem to enjoy it, and go again and again to each successive flower, well knowing what the result will be, and apparently "touching off the trigger" without a tremor, or even holding their breath. But they and their foreparents for thousands of years have got accustomed to it, and I half imagine that the baby bee, even in his first visit to one of these blossoms, knows precisely what will happen. Pop! pop! go the exploding flowers, one after the other, at each touch of the bee, throwing up a cloud of yellow pollen which covers the bodies of the insects until they are as dusty as little millers.

There is an endless variety in these various welcomes among the flowers, and our barberry has one of the queerest of them all. Poets of all ages have loved to dwell upon the flowers—their "swete smels," exquisite forms, fragrance, and colors. The droning bees in an environment of fragrant bloom have moved many a poetic pen to inspiration. But it is not often that the bards have seen deep enough into the floral mysteries to immortalize the *doings* of the blossoms.

I recall one such allusion, however, with reference to this mischievous blossom of the barberry. How well old Hosea Biglow knew its pranks!

"All down the loose-walled lanes in archin' bowers
The barb'ry droops its strings o' golden flowers,
Whose shrinkin' hearts the school-gals love to try
With *pins*. They'll worry yourn so, boys, bime-by."

Those "shrinkin' hearts" of the barberry blossom, so long the wonder and amusement of children, including many children of adult growth, have, so far as I know, herein found their first and only historian—historian, but not interpreter. For Hosea Biglow, nor his literary parent, James Russell Lowell, never dreamed of the significance of this strange spectacle in the shrinkin' hearts of the barberry bloom when surprised with the point of a pin.

But the bee can tell us all about it. He has known this singular trick in the barberry for ages, and kept the secret all to himself. Only comparatively recently (1859 or thereabouts) did the secret leak out, when Darwin, by the previous hints of several other philosophers, discovered the key which unlocked the mystery of this as well as thousands of other similar riddles among the flowers.

These strange "manners" of the blossoms had then a deep vital principle at their base. They had not *always* been thus, but had gradually, through long ages of time, changed and modified their shapes, colors, odors, nectar, and their manners for one purpose—*to insure* their pollen

"In archin' bowers"

being conveyed away upon the bodies of insects and carried to a *second* flower, and there placed upon the stigma to insure fertilization and development of the seed.

The plans, devices, tricks, and pranks by which flowers accomplish this result are past belief. I have indicated only a few by way of a hint, and in previous papers on the bluebottle and figwort have described others, but none quite similar to the barberry.

We all know the barberry, the prickly, thorny

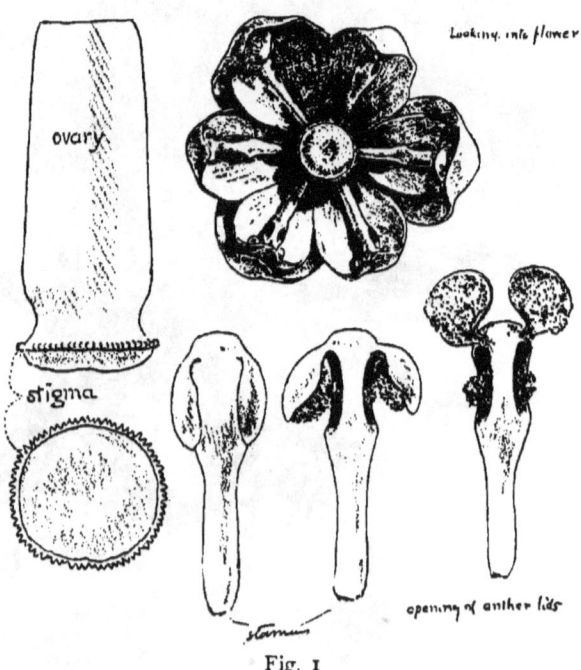

Fig. 1

barberry, whether with its "strings o' golden flowers" or its drooping clusters of brilliant scarlet acid berries. But each one of those berries is but a token of a bee's visit, as we shall presently see. At Fig. 1 I have shown a plan of the barberry blossom seen from below, its yellow sepals and petals open, and opposite each of the inner set, and pressed against it, a stamen. This stamen is shown below in three stages — closed, partly open, and fully open — the queer little ear-shaped lids finally drawn up, showing the pollen-pockets, and also withdrawing a portion of the pollen from the cavity. At the centre is seen the circular tip of the ovary which finally becomes the berry — that is, when the little scheme here planned has been fulfilled. This circular form represents the tip of the ovary, and the little toothed rim the *stigma*. Now what is the intention here expressed? This construction represents a plan, first, to invite a bee—this is done by its color, its fragrance, and its nectar, which is secreted in a gland at the base of each petal, near the centre of the flower; secondly, to make that bee bear away the pollen; thirdly, to cause that same bee to place this pollen on the stigma rim of the next flower he visits. In Fig. 2 we see how beautifully this plan is carried out by the insect, without his suspecting how perfectly he has been utilized. At A we see the same flower cut open sideways, the waiting, expectant stamens tucked away at the sides, leaving a free opening to the base of the flower. Now comes our bee. He must needs hang back downward to sip at the

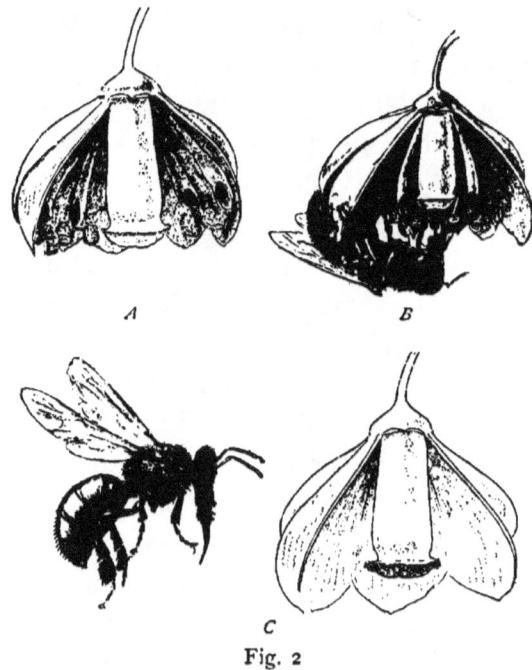

Fig. 2

drooping flower. As his tongue enters, and finally touches the base of these stamens, *clap!* they come one after another against his tongue and face, and there deposit their load of pollen (B). The bee, who has doubtless got over his surprise at this demonstration — if, indeed, he ever had any — now flies to another blossom, perhaps on the same cluster (C). Entering it as before, the notched edge of the stigmatic rim comes in contact with the pollen on his tongue and face, and the flower is thus fertilized by pollen from another barberry blossom, the intention of the flower now perfectly realized in *cross*-fertilization.

The seeds from *cross*-fertilized flowers are almost invariably more vigorous, and thus yield more vigorous plants, than those of flowers fertilized with their own *pollen*, and this is why most flowers have necessarily developed some means by which cross-fertilization can be secured. And this has been done through evolution working on the lines of *natural* selection, those seedlings which had originally happened, by a variation in the flower, to be thus favored by some chance peculiarity which insured cross-fertilization, winning in the struggle with the previous weaker individuals, and finally supplanting them altogether.

A Woolly Flock

HARDLY a season passes without my being in receipt of one or more inquiries, personal or by letter, concerning this snowy brood which haunts the alders in the swamp or along the road-side, and which envelops the smaller branches in its dense, feathery fringe. It is often one of the most frequent and conspicuous incidents in a country walk during its season, and its season ranges from its height in early summer until the frost. And yet how few there are, even of those, perhaps, who pass it every day, who have any definite idea of its character!

I know one rustic who claimed that it was "dry-rot," or a "speeshy of mould"; but the woolly phenomenon is commonly dismissed by the rural mind with the observation that it is "bugs of some sort." In this case the haphazard verdict happens to be the literal truth, though the speaker little suspects how closely he has discriminated. But his present skill is easily accounted for when we remember that only yesterday he had a great deal to say about "June-bugs" and "lightning-bugs." He will tell you all about "lady-bugs," too, and "rose-bugs," and "horn-bugs," and "pinch-bugs"—and has he not often given his strong opinion on "potato-bugs"?—not one of which insects is in the least entitled to the name of "bug." Only this very morning he asked me if I was "as fond of goin' buggin' as I used to be." But to the granger laity the entomologist is always a "bug-hunter," even though no single species of a bug is to be found in his entire insect cabinet.

What, then, is a bug, and why is the discrimination of "bugs of some sort" so truly applicable to this brood with the snowy wool which grows upon the alder twigs?

The term "bug" has almost become a popular synonym for "insect." All bugs *are* insects, 'tis true, but it by no means follows that all insects are bugs. The "squash-bug" is almost the only insect that is known by its true title in the popular vocabulary, for this disgusting insect is in truth a typical bug.

But who would ever think of calling the whizzing harvest-fly a "bug?" Rather will they persist that he is a "locust," which he is not. He should be called the cicada. The "grasshopper" of the fields is the true locust, whose swarms of certain species in the Orient have so often shut out the sun, and whose voracious feeding has laid waste whole square miles of vegetation in a single night.

But such a swarm of locusts as we read of in Scripture, and frequently in the history of modern times and in our own country, would be comparatively tame and merely amusing affairs were they composed of our so-called "locust"—he of the whizzing timbrel in the sultry August noon. For this insect has no teeth, and could not bite a blade of grass if it wanted to. And herein we see one of the peculiarities which constitute him a "bug," and which also includes in the same company our woolly swarm upon the alder twigs. In place of teeth these insects are supplied with a beak for sucking the juices of plants. If we carefully examine the dense snowy mass we find it composed of small tufts closely crowded together, each tuft being borne upon the plump body of a small insect whose beak is deeply sunk into the tender bark.

I have separated one of the little creatures, and furnished his portrait as he appears when viewed through a magnifying-glass, only the lower portion of his body being covered with the wool, his head and legs being usually concealed beneath the pluming growth of his neighbors. This feathery growth seems of the most delicate consistency—in truth, more suggestive of white "mould" than any other natural substance, and seems to proceed from pores in the plump body beneath it. The slightest breath wafts the cobwebby tips of the fringe, and the least rude touch easily dislodges it, exposing the round, naked body of what is now clearly seen to be an aphis, or plant-louse, which nature, for some reason, has seen fit to clothe with swan's-down.

In early June the white down first appears on the alders in tiny patches here and there. This gradually extends down the stem, at length, perhaps, completely encircling it, and thus remaining for weeks, the full-grown aphis at last attaining a length of about three-sixteenths of an inch.

A similar brood is sometimes seen in profusion on beech-trees and also on the apple-tree. But if we imagine that because these insects are without teeth they are therefore harmless, we are greatly mistaken. What they lack in individual effect they fully compensate for in numbers, and the combined attack of a girdle of thousands of these sucking beaks, for weeks absorbing the sap, may often result in the death of the branch beyond them.

Dr. Harris, in his admirable work on " Insects Injurious to Vegetation," tells us that " in Gloucestershire, England, so many apple-trees were destroyed by these lice in the year 1810 that the making of cider had to be abandoned. So infested were many of the trees that they seemed, at a short distance, as if they had been whitewashed."

Other insects, such as the flea and the mosquito, are also possessed of similar " beaks for sucking," but neither of these examples is a bug, both being *flies*—the flea merely a wingless fly with wonderfully developed legs. Our entomology tells us that a bug is a member of the *Hemiptera*, meaning " half-winged;" the wings of the typical bug, like the squash-bug, being transparent for only about half their length. But as in the flea among flies, here we find myriads of true bugs without a vestige of wings, and others, like the cicada, with ample wings as clear and free from opacity as those of a fly. It would take more space than I have at disposal to tell precisely what a bug really is entomologically, such a diversity of

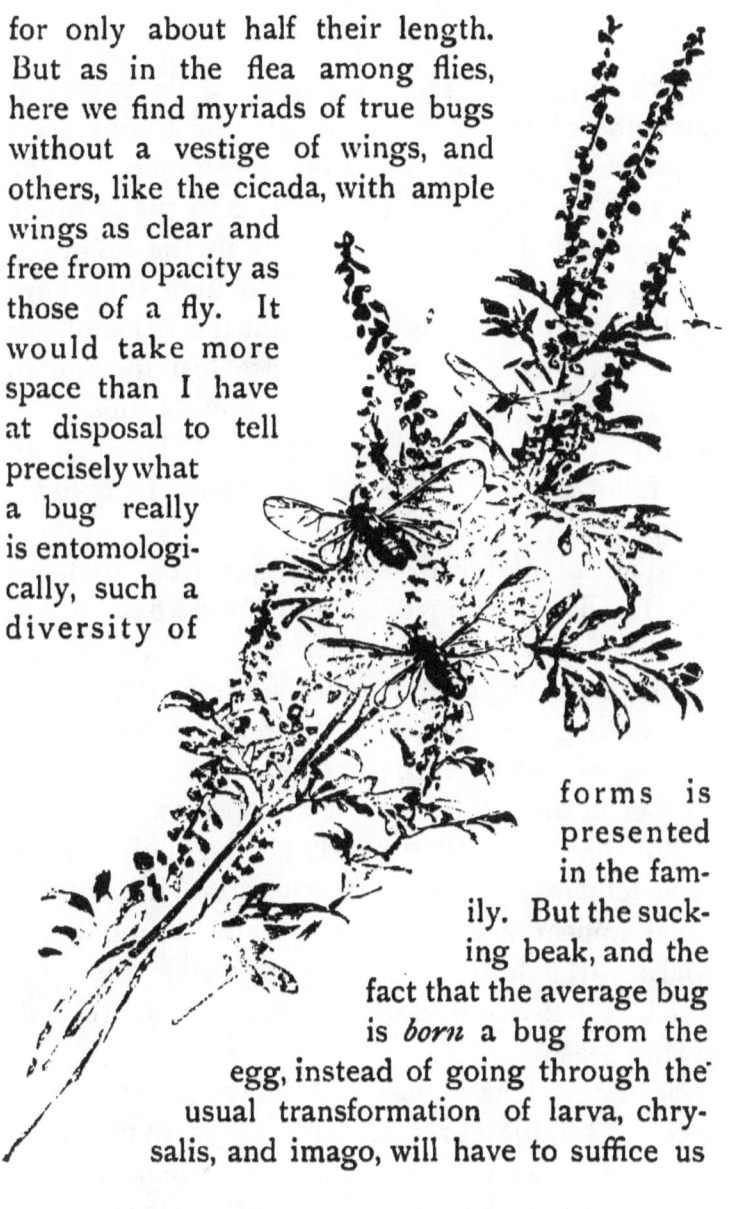

forms is presented in the family. But the sucking beak, and the fact that the average bug is *born* a bug from the egg, instead of going through the usual transformation of larva, chrysalis, and imago, will have to suffice us for the present. Here, for instance, is the great sub-tribe of the aphis, to which our woolly specimen belongs. What is their life history? The eggs of the mother aphis are laid in the autumn, giving birth to the baby swarm in the following spring. In an almost incredible time they have multiplied to such an extent that the twigs of our roses and many other plants are lost to view in the encircling swarm. The secret of this wonderful arithmetical progression may be seen in the following quotation, which applies to aphides in general:

"The plant-louse of the apple-tree produces one hundred young ones in a single generation, these being born alive, and each of these brings forth others in equal number, until, at the end of the tenth generation, which is reached before the coming of frost, the original aphis has become the mother of one quintillion of her species."

But up to this time nearly all the aphides have been females; in the last generation the winged males appear, and are seen assembled among the swarm—the last mother brood laying the eggs which are to start anew the cycle of life the following season.

So far as I have observed, however, the woolly species of aphis never acquires wings, nature having in a measure compensated for their absence in the growth of plumy down, which, according to

Harris, is so buoyant as to enable the insect to be borne upon the breeze from tree to tree. To this resource he attributes the spread of the wingless apple-lice species. But it would take a stiff breeze thus to waft the body of our plump dweller on the alder, unless, indeed, in his younger days.

"What Ails him"

ON a certain afternoon last August, having just completed a particularly laborious work upon which I had long been engaged, and with my mind naturally inclined towards relaxation in my plans for the morrow's labors, my eye instinctively sought a certain note-book upon my table. It was a note-book containing memoranda on a wide variety of Nature topics, but presented in a particular place a choice, selected list of topics under the title of "Young People." A large number of these memoranda were crossed off with a pencil line, which told me that these particular topics had already served their purpose, were sufficiently elaborated in the columns of the "Young People," and were now safely preserved between the covers of my book "Sharp Eyes."

But what an array of items were still left from the winnowing, which had after all culled only a few of the best! Indeed, it was hard to decide which should be selected as the subject for the morrow. Let's see; shall it be those travelling underground buds of the Clintoma, with all their leaves and flowers ready for next spring? No, I must wait a little for these a month later and they will be more mature, and I must make my drawing from nature. Then there is that queer blue oil beetle, with his queerer history; that slender-waisted wasp that digs its deep hole in the dirt, and those round holes in the path, with their mysterious hocus-pocus.

Yes, it shall be these, the magic holes that disappear as you cautiously look at them, or suddenly start into view as you approach — deep holes, the diameter of a slate-pencil, with apparently nothing in them, but which in reality have a good deal of mischief at the bottom of them or at the top of them, as it happens. "Ant holes," most people call them. Many an ant, doubtless, goes into them, but not because he wants to. "Yes," I thought, "my next chapter shall be devoted to these queer holes and their shy tenants, which so few people ever see or even dream of."

Having thus decided, I closed my note-book, but the experience of the next few minutes quite reversed my plans, and led to the completion of an entirely different article, or the pictures for it at least, on the same afternoon, without awaiting the morrow.

I had barely closed the note-book when, chancing to glance out of my studio window, I observed a well-known neighbor, a thrifty, retired granger and carpenter, approaching across lots. His house stood out against the sky at the crest of the slope, about a furlong distant, above my studio, and he had perhaps reached half-way to my window before I had observed him. Something in his walk, his somewhat accelerated pace and evident preoccupied mood, as well as a peculiar position of his extended right hand, foretold that some unusual errand had turned his steps hitherward. With considerable curiosity I endeavored to detect at a distance the specimen which he was bringing, well knowing from experience that I should soon recognize an old friend, which for sixty years had somehow managed to escape the notice of its new discoverer.

Half across the meadow I now observed that he held a leaf in his outstretched hand, and now I clearly noted that it was a compound leaf, and in another second I knew it all. For was it not a leaf of the Virginia-creeper or woodbine? and how many before him have marvelled at that strange exhibition among the woodbine leaves which had now probably met his eyes for the first time? In another moment he was at the piazza stoop, and now he appears at the studio door. Eager anticipation and shortness of breath were equally manifest as he approached my easel and, with his right hand still outstretched towards me, exclaimed, "Well, what ails *him*?"

at the same time laying down before me the mysterious specimen. It was a leaf of the woodbine, bearing along its stem a cylindrical mass of what appeared to be tiny, oblong, white eggs, all set on end, and so densely packed that but for the head and tail of the shrunken, green caterpillar which appeared at the two extremities of the mass no one would have guessed their origin. "What ails him?"

"I was sitting on my porch," continued my puzzled visitor, "and saw the white thing among the leaves, and took a closer look at it, and found it was this. I never saw anything like it before, and I thought perhaps you hadn't either, or, at least, that if you had you could tell me something about it. What ails him, anyhow?"

The story was simply told, and my readers who have followed my articles already know what the story is. We remember the strange history of those little, puzzling cocoon clusters on a grass stem, those " bewitched cocoons " which gave birth to swarms of tiny wasps instead of moths, and we realize that here is more of the same sort of mischief, all of which I explained to my good neighbor, to his astonishment. How a few weeks since, when our caterpillar was much smaller than now, a tiny, black midget hovered about him, and, in spite of all his wriggling and squirming, stung him again and again, each time inserting within his body its tiny eggs. Perhaps, and probably in this case, from the number of the white tokens, more than one of the flies took a turn at the unlucky victim, for he certainly seems to have got more than his share.

"These eggs thus inserted beneath the skin of the caterpillar," I explained, " soon hatched into minute white grubs, which immediately fastened themselves upon the tissues within the caterpillar's body, and he is now obliged to eat for the whole family, which he continues to do without any outward signs of inconvenience or protest, which, of course, would be useless. I fancy he must have frequent attacks of that 'all-gone' feeling that we hear so much about in dyspeptic people, but if he does he gives no hint of it by his looks, as he devours one leaf after another along the stem, and displays his plump proportions with evident pride—like the whole tribe of horny-tailed 'sphinx' caterpillars to which he belongs.

"But a few days ago he had a sudden and terrible experience. He had begun to think of retiring down among the dried leaves on the ground and spinning a cocoon, and there were bright visions of a future life filling his little green head— visions of a life on wings, as quick as thought, in an atmosphere of twilight and fragrance, and all manner of sweet indulgences. But his beautiful dream was interrupted, and probably will remain only as a dream. At one moment we see him in his prime, a perfect specimen for the 'bug-hunter' who is after the larva of *Chærocampa pampinatrix*. In ten minutes we look at him again: we find his body shrunken and covered with minute white grubs, all standing on their tails, which are still imbedded in his body; here one barely emerged; here another half enshrouded in a gauzy cocoon; others with their bodies bent into loops weaving the webby gauze about them, while a few hours hence all are concealed, as we see them now, in the completed long, oval, white cocoons which still remain attached to his body."

"Well," remarked my listener, "I guess he feels pretty sick; if he don't, I vow I feel sick for him. I knew something awful ailed him, but didn't know what. I thought the things were eggs. What's the good of it all, anyhow? What do the cocoons turn into?"

I have wished more than once that my friend could have been in my studio the day following his visit, in order to have witnessed the ocular answer to his last question. It was evident that his caterpillar specimen might have been discovered with its load of cocoons a fortnight ago, for in the morning, upon opening the box in which I had placed him, a number of tiny black flies flew out, and several of the white cocoons were open at the end, their dainty hinged lids thrown back. Here is one with its black midge just creeping out; others with the tiny imp peeping through the fine crevice; others with the lid still tightly closed, but with its juncture disclosing more distinctly every moment the knavery of the busy teeth within. One by one the silken lids popped up, and out flew the mischievous jack-in-the-box until within the space of a few hours every cocoon was empty. So this is "what ailed him." He has been the victim of the parasitic fly known as *microgaster*.

But even now that his mortal enemies have left him, I fancy he is past encouragement or salvation. What will become of him? In his particular case he continued to dwindle and soon died, though in other instances I have known him to recover and reach the chrysalis stage, to complete his transformation into a beautiful olive and red sphinx-moth.

The Cicada's Last Song

UNDER the popular name of "locust," our cicada, or harvest-fly, has long enjoyed the reputation as our chief insect musician, vying with the katydid in the volume of its song. We all know its long, whizzing crescendo in the sultry summer days. But let us call things by their right names. This buzzing musician is *not* a *locust;* it is a *cicada*. The true locust is what we ordinarily call a grasshopper, that "high-elbowed grig" of the meadows, so generous with his "molasses," and with such a vigorous kick. He, too, is a musician in a modest way—a fiddler, carrying his "fiddle" on the edge of his folded wing covers, against which he gently grinds out faint, squeaky music, using his thigh-joint as a fiddle-bow. His single efforts are barely audible, but multiplied ten-thousandfold in his great field orchestra, becomes a murmur which may be distinctly heard, and which no doubt all of us have heard without a suspicion as to its source. It is a part of the great musical symphony of the harvest-fields, a roundel sustained and prolonged by the hum of bees and the buzzing of innumerable flies, and the sprightly notes of crickets, attuned to the soft murmur of breeze-blown grass. This meadow music is perceptible to any one who cares to listen for it, but it is rarely noticed. What we call the "quiet" country life, or "the quiet summer noon" of the poet, is a misnomer.

The contrast, to the observant ear, between the meadow in a hot July noon and the same meadow on a following cool and overcast day would be remarkable could we but compare the two conditions during the same moment of time. Even a cloud shadow passing over a "quiet" meadow will often suddenly reveal to us how *noisy* it really was but a moment before. But the harsh timbrel of the cicada is not a part of this "quiet" music. He is no retiring fiddler hiding somewhere among the grass-blades. His note rings out high above the meadow chorus, and he always gets the credit as the chief soloist, and we say, "Hark! there's a 'locust,'" when we ought to know better. Let us try and straighten out this confusion of terms, and let the younger generation at least begin the reform that shall eventually set matters right and correct this wide-spread popular error.

Our cicada belongs to quite another family of insects. Instead of jaws for biting, as our fiddling "grasshopper," the cicada has only a long "beak for sucking," and this feature alone connects him with the tribe of "bugs." Moreover, his methods of music-making are very different from those of the "grasshopper" tribe. It is the male only that makes the music, and his instrument is a drum. He carries two of these inclosed within his body, the opening of each being covered beneath by a broad plate, which is easily seen on the under surface of the body. Deep within lies the "drum," and the hard and hollow body of the insect acts as a resonator or sounding-board. This drummer does not use his legs as drum-sticks, as might be supposed, his drum being vibrated by twitching muscles and cords.

The method by which the sound is produced may be illustrated by a simple experiment. Take a small piece of stiff, sized writing-paper or smooth Manilla paper, and by pressure with some rounded blunt instrument produce a slight hollow or blister upon its surface. Upon pressure from either side this blister will be found to "snap," and could we but repeat the operation with great rapidity, a continuous sound would result. The toy called the "telegraph ticker" is made on this principle, the blister being made on a strip of steel, and the click produced by pressure upon its top, the elasticity of the metal bringing it back to its original position of rest, and each motion accompanied by a snap as the blister changes sides. Indeed, we need look no further than the bottom of almost any well-ordered tin pan for a complete illustration of this principle. So our cicada is a drummer, and his favorite tune is a "roll-call," the beats following each other with such rapidity as to form a tone. All through the summer we hear his strain. Even at this moment, as I write, a very long-winded specimen is tuning up in the tree just outside my studio window, and I am almost moved to give him some good advice. Have a care, my noisy minstrel. If it were I alone who were within ear-shot of your noise all might be well with you, but there are others near by to whom your music hath charms. Have a care! Only a moment ago I heard an ominous hum on my piazza, and upon investigation discovered a huge sand-hornet prying about the premises. He knows what he is looking for, and so ought you, if your parents have done their duty by you. Hereditary instinct at least ought to teach you that your drum should play second fiddle to that hornet's humming music. I remember once being the witness of the sad fate of an ancestor of yours who drummed not wisely but too well. He was monopolizing the neighborhood, just as you are doing now, when I noticed his principal effort was suddenly cut short in the middle in a most unusual manner. If he had been a singer I would have supposed some rival had clapped a hand over his mouth, so suddenly was the song abbreviated. In another moment there was a rustling among the leaves, as something fell from the tree in his immediate neighborhood. Down, down it dropped, its passage to the ground accompanied by one or two short, sharp, spasmodic tattoos on that same noisy drum. The object fell among some rocks, but before I could reach the spot the humming sound of a sand-hornet greeted my ears, and in a moment more the insect took flight directly across my path, and, what was more, he was not alone. Would you know who accompanied him? Look then on the picture on page 252, and have a care, my noisy friend, for the lineal descendant of that sand-hornet now hovers outside my doorway. He has a grudge against your tribe, and he is even now on your scent. Perhaps you may be interested to know what the hornet did with that rash ancestor of yours. Well, I will tell you, for your own good. Guided by his noisy demonstration, the hornet spied him on his twig, and in a second had pounced upon him and, like a highwayman, stabbed him to the heart with a poisoned javelin. This cut short his song, as you may well suppose, and he fell in the grasp of his assailant. In another moment the hornet got a fresh hold upon him, and though your ancestor, like yourself, was much bigger than the hornet, those powerful, buzzing wings made an easy burden of him for quite a distance across the meadow. Here our captor took a rest, and after tugging that helpless cicada some distance up a high fence-rail, started off on another flight, which was brought to an end in the grass at the foot of a tree. In a moment more the hornet was seen tugging its huge load up the trunk. When some ten feet in height a third flight was made, this time gradually settling down on the roof of a shed down-hill. Tugging his game to the edge of the shed roof, a fourth trip was made, and this landed the two in the neighborhood of a sand bank at the roadside in the valley below.

A sand bank of some sort is usually the terminus of this strange ride of the cicada. Thus far many curious observers have followed the two, and wondered what it was all about. If they had cared to follow the matter to the end, they would

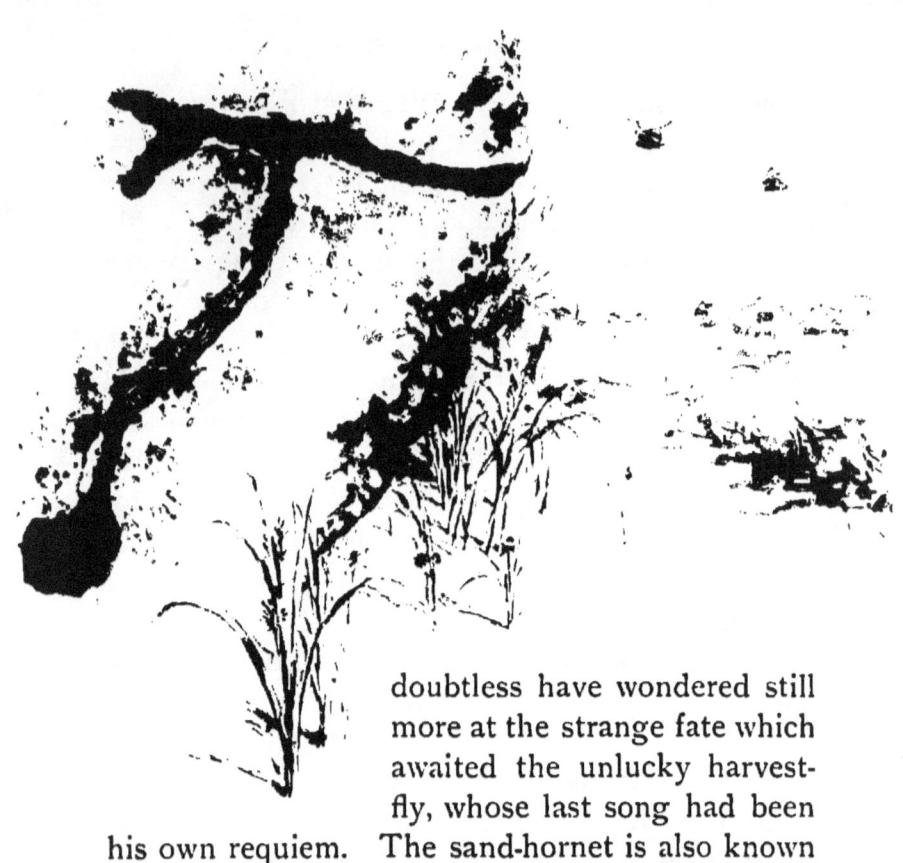

doubtless have wondered still more at the strange fate which awaited the unlucky harvest-fly, whose last song had been his own requiem. The sand-hornet is also known as the "digger-wasp," the largest of its kind, the most formidable of all our hornets, and carrying within its black, yellow-spotted body a most searching and terrible poisoned sting. It was a common belief in ancient times that "seventeen pricks of a hornet" would "kill a man," to quote from Pliny; and there are many country people to-day who would as quickly attack a rattlesnake as this big sand-hornet, and who "absolutely know" of men who have been "knocked down" and even "killed" by one stab of its sting. However this may be, it is well to keep at a respectful distance. When we know what the little yellow-jacket can do with its tiny dagger, and then reflect that this sand-hornet's javelin is about a third of an inch long, we can draw our own conclusions, and will readily understand why it was that our cicada's song was cut short. "But why didn't the hornet eat him on the spot? Why should it fly away with him and yank him about so unmercifully?" This is a common question with those who have observed the episode above described. A visit to the sand bank would have explained the object of it all. The exposed surface is seen to be perforated here and there with holes as large as one's little finger, while from one of them an occasional tiny stream of sand pours out, and we catch a glimpse of the horny, spiked legs of the digger-wasp within. Even as we observe him closely a loud hum is heard, and a filmy, buzzing object falls precipitately upon the bank, and in the jumble of wings and black bodies we now distinguish our hornet and cicada, which only a moment before had started from the edge of the shed roof above. The cicada is apparently dead, and is now an easy prey as the wasp lugs him to the mouth of one of the burrows, and soon disappears in its depths.

Further than this few have followed the couple. But Professor C. V. Riley, our government entomologist, has unearthed the entire mystery, and eye-witnessed the fate of our cicada, and I am thus enabled to picture the rest of the tragedy. What now follows is very similar to what I described in a previous paper concerning the mud-wasp nest packed with its dead spiders. Our cicada is not dead—more's the pity. The thrust of the sting has only paralyzed the insect, in order that the young of the hornet may be provided with *living* food. From the opening of the tunnel in the sand our harvest-fly was lugged a distance of about six inches, when the tunnel branched in various directions. Down a branch for about eight inches more, and his journey terminated in a dungeon, where his career was doomed to end. Doubtless each of the other branches held one or two similar prisoners, for the cicada is the favorite prey of this particular wasp. Once arrived at the dungeon, the hornet deposits an egg upon its victim, and leaves him in its charge. In a few days it hatches into a larva with such a voracious appetite that within a week it has devoured the contents of the cicada's shell and reached its full growth. It now incloses itself within a silky cocoon, and after abiding the winter emerges at the brim in the spring a full-fledged hornet, with its mouth watering at the thought of cicadas.

What a strange wonder-working medicine is this which the hornet carries in its laboratory! In the guise of death it yet prolongs life indefi-

nitely. The ordinary existence of the cicada, for instance, is but a few weeks at most, and yet it is claimed by Mr. Riley that if for any reason the egg of the wasp should fail to hatch, the paralyzed cicada will remain in its condition of suspended animation for a year, and presumably longer.

Here is a suggestion for the materia medica

which may open up immortal fame to the chemist of the future. What is this mysterious essence which the wasp carries in its poniard? As Professor Riley suggestively remarks, "If man could do what these wasps have done from time immemorial, viz., preserve for an indefinite period the animals they feed on by the simple insertion of some toxic fluid in the tissues, he would be able to revolutionize the present methods of shipping cattle and sheep, and obviate much of the cruelty which now attends the transportation of live-stock and much of the expense involved in cold storage."

INDEX

ACRID buttercup leaves, 10.
Agaric, 142, 144.
Alders, leaf-rolling beetles of, 233.
Amanita muscarius, 142; print from, 143.
American velvet plant, 25.
Andrena bee, 222.
Andromeda-bell, its welcome to the bee, 221, 222.
Aniline bath, 47.
Aphides, 125, 126; pest of the rose-garden; plants and trees, 126; sucking the sap, 127; disappearance of a swarm, 128; all females; end of season males appear; wonderful multiplication of, 233, 236.
Aphis lion (*Hemorobida*), 128, 129.
Aphrophora, "spume-bearer," 89.
Apple-trees bearing pumpkins and squashes, 192.
Aquilegia canadensis, columbine, 46.
Arachne, 106.
Archippus. See Butterflies.
Argiope riparia, ballooning or flying spiders, 120.

Artists as interpreters of the beauty of the commonplace, 26.
Asters, 110.
Attacus prometheus, 75.
Aurelias, 161.

BALLOON, the true, 118.
Ballooning spiders (*Argiope riparia*), annual picnic of, 114; shooting of webs, 115; sailing out of sight; sending out broad bands from their spinnerets, 117; skilful handling, 118; making the balloon; the ascension; manner of alighting, 119.
Baltimore oriole, 172.
Banquet of beetles, 134.
Barberry blossoms, shrinking hearts; strange manners, 224; an unsuspecting agent, 227.
Bedegnar, sponge-gall, 43.
Bees:—bumble, 6, 91; honey, 7; yellow-jacket, 91; *Andrena*, 222.
Beetles:—floundering, 1; tiger (*Cicindelidæ*), oil, 2; snapping (*Elater*),

INDEX

20; perfumed (*Osmoderma scabei*), 133; blue oil, 239.
Bellworts, 44.
Bigelow, Hosea, quoted, 224.
Billings, Josh, quoted, 92, 124.
Birds'-nests, materials of:—milkweed bark, toad-skins, and snake-skins, 171, 172; twine and horsehair, caterpillar-skins, 172; wool, dandelion seeds, 173; gray lichens and seeds, 177.
Black-paper hornet, his bad reputation, 94; a tempting target; results of an attack on his house, 96; making themselves promiscuous; the stoical bachelor, 97; his discomfiture, 98; antics explained; his hiding-place revealed, 100; favorite hunting-ground, 101; occasional big game; life of; manner of laying eggs; several broods in a season, 102; number of tiers in a nest; winter the best time to examine nests, 103.
Black snake, 85.
Blossom etiquette, 221, 222.
Blue carnation, 46.
Blue dahlia, 45.
Blue oil beetle, 239.
Blue pansies, 46.
Blue rose, 45, 46.
Blue tulip, 45.
Bluets, *Houstonia*, 24, 208, 209.
Boletus, 142.
Bridge-building spiders, 104.
Brooklyn Bridge, 104; "carrier" or "traveller" should have been called "spider," 105; Engineer Farrington crossing, 110.
Brown screech-owl, 151.

Browning, Robert, quoted, 26.
"Bull's-eye" caterpillar, 156.
Bumble-bee, 6, 91.
Butterflies asleep at night, 168.
Butterflies:—Idalia (*Argynnis idalia*), Archippus (*Danais archippus*), yellow swallow-tails (*Papilio turnus*), 131; Red Admiral (*Vanessa Atalanta*), 155, 158, 161; "comma" (*Vanessa comma*), 156, 161, 170; Atalanta (*Cynthia Atalanta*), 158; semicolon (*Vanessa interrogationis*), 161.

CANTERBURY bells, 42.
Cardanus quoted, 93.
Careless observation of nature, 185, 186.
Carnation, blue, 46.
Catbrier, 188.
Caterpillars:—woolly-bear (*Arctiadæ*), 148; "bull's-eye" (*Saturnia Io*), 156; sphinx (*Chærocampa panipenatrix*, 241.
Cecropia, 156.
Chinese pink, 73.
Chipmonk, 153.
Chrysalids, 161.
Chrysanthemum, 86, 127.
Cicada, 87, 246; his manner of feeding; how he differs from the grasshopper; the secret of his music, 250; his last song; borne off by his captor, 251; living food, 254; suspended animation, 255.
Clintonia, 239.
Clothes moth (*Tineidæ*), 170.
Clover (*Trifolium*), four-leaved, 215; nine-leaved, found in groups, 216; possibilities of cultivation, 217; an exceptional find, 218,

INDEX

219; saying its prayers, 219; lotus, 222.
Cobweb showers, 114; blinding dogs interrupting sport, 114; flakes and rags of, 115; silken streamers, 116; shower in Prospect Park, Brooklyn, 120; on Brooklyn Bridge, 121.
Cocoons:—curious, 145; solid to the core, 147; ribs and vertebræ, 149; secret of the hollow, 151; what the pellets were, 152; yielding wasps, 242.
Colors of flowers, laws governing colors and combinations, 44, 45; natural exception to; three primary colors in the hyacinth, Egyptian lotus; sky reflections destroying color, 45.
Columbine (*Aquilegia canadensis, A. chrysantha, A. cærulea*), puzzling color classification, from white through all shades of red, yellow, and blue, 46.
"Comma." See Butterflies.
Coral, gray, 73.
Cow-spittle, 84, 86.
Crickets, 71.
Cross-fertilization of flowers, 30, 167, 208, 211, 229.
Cuban belle's toilet, 21.
Culpepper, Dr., quoted, 154.
Cyanic, flowers with all shades of blue and red without yellow, 45.
Cynips seminator, Cynips rosæ, gall-flies, 40.

DAHLIA, blue, 45.
Daisy, pesky white weed, almost identical with the marguerite, 25; a marvel of a flower, 28, 205, 211.
Dandelion. Seeds used for birds'-nests, 173; mutilation of, 174; a week of retirement, 175; flight of the seed-bed, 176; the burglar discovered, 177, 211.
Darwin, 202, 209, 224.
Darwin flowers, 166, 167, 168.
De Candolle. Color limitations in flowers, 45, 202.
Deer-mouse, 151.
Desmodium, 223.
"Digger-wasps," sand-hornets, 252.
Dungeons of death, 54.

EGYPTIAN history, 53.
Egyptian yellow lotus, 45.
Evening primrose (*Œnothera biennis*), 85; luminous blossoms of, 163; daylight mystery; seeds, pods, and caterpillars, 164; curious secret; two buds, 165; primrose blooms for moths, 168; blighted buds, 169; a poor recompense, 170.

FAIRY sponges, the growth of; rich colors of sweetbrier sponge, 38, 42; contents of the sponge, 42.
False scorpions (*Pedipalpi*), 181; among old books and papers; born rovers, 182.
Figwort (*Scrophularia*), tall and spindling, purplish-olive blossoms; odor of; food for wasps, 28; fertilized by wasps; bud open in the morning; flowers change from day to day, 30; growth of the ovary, 32.
Flies:—gall, 40; lace-wing, 122; gold-banded, 129; house, 178;

INDEX

laphria, 182; ichneumon, 196; parasitic, 200; harvest, 87, 246.

Floundering beetle, color of, 1; funny characteristics of; leaking habits, 2; playing possum, 3; feats of; diminutive size when young; golden-yellow case, 4; number of joints, 5; a snug resting-place; first outing, 6; in the bee hotel; transformation, 8; in the mummy-case; change of diet, 10.

Fly-fungus, 184.

Flying-machine, toy, 117.

Fox-fire, a column of phosphorescence, of greenish, ghostly hue, 12; prosaic fence-post; effect of a reflection of lantern in water, 13; feeding on darkness, 14; short life of, 15; village spook; haunted mill, 16; a night terror, 18; six square feet of brilliancy, 19; yeast as a possible cause; dead fish; curious effect from decaying potatoes, 20; phosphorus not always present; burnt oyster-shells in combination with certain acids; the supposed secret of, 22; decoy for deer; the largest on record, 23.

Frog-hoppers, 89.

Frog-spit, 84, 89.

GALL-FLY (*Cynips seminator, Cynips rosæ*), 40; a cousin to the wasps; magician in chemistry, 41.

Genista, 223.

Geometrical web-makers, 120.

Ghost-fire, 15.

Gold-banded flower-fly, larva of, 129.

Gossamer showers, 113.

Gramatophora trisignata, "Professor Wiggler," 81, 82.

Grape-vine, 186-194.

Grasshoppers, 71, 195; "Quakers;" camp-meeting ground, 197; a paralyzed specimen; unnatural movements, 198; a transparent body, 199; a swarm of flies, 200; 246.

Green roses, 187.

Grew, Nehemias, 205.

HANG-BIRD, 172.

Harris, "Insects Injurious to Vegetation," quoted, 89, 134, 233, 237.

Harvest-fly, 87, 246.

Hawthorne's fox-fire, 19, 23.

"History of Selborne," 114.

Hollyhock, 45.

Honey-dew, 126.

Honey-sippers, 221.

Hornet, 87, 92; as mad as, 93; always on the rampage, 94, 100, 102.

Horse-hair snakes, New England farmers' idea of the origin of; stories of, 65; flying over the meadows in haying time, 66; two specimens in alcohol, 69; what was found in a bait-box, 71.

"Hot-foot," 92.

House-fly (*Musca domestica*), his never-ending toilet, 178; a curious tag, 179; live young lobster, strength of his grip, 180; his many enemies; abundant use for all his eyes, 182; September and October danger months; the white nimbus; acute dyspepsia, 183.

Houstonia, bluets, 208, 209.

Hunters, 161.

Hyacinth, 45.

ICHNEUMON flies, 196.

INDEX

Idalia. See Butterflies.

JIBING neighbors, 68.
Johnny-jumper, 46.
Jussieu, 202.

KEATS, JOHN, quoted, 164.

LACE-WING fly (*Chrysopa oculata*):—
Color of eyes and wings, 122;
lasting odor; ways of the gauzy
sprite, 123; method of egg-laying;
born in a land of plenty, 124; a
voracious appetite; tubular teeth,
126.
Lady-bug, larva of, 129.
" Laphria-fly," 182.
Lilac-bushes, 75.
Lindley, 202.
Linnæus, 202, 206.
Locust, 232, 246.
Lotus clover, 222.
Lovelorn maiden, 213.
Lowell, James Russell, 224.

McCOOK, Rev. Dr., quoted, 110-118.
Meadow contrasts, 247.
Mignonette, 204.
Monk's-hood blossom, 205.
Morning gossamer, 112.
Moths:—Polyphemus (*Telea polyphemus*), *Attacus prometheus*,
75, 196; Trisignata (*Gramatophora trisignata*), 81; *Cecropia*, Bull's-
eye (*Saturnia Io*), 156; twilight moth; common clothes moth
(*Tineidæ*), 170.
Mullein (*Verbascum thrapsus*), 25.
Mummy-cases, 54.
Mushrooms, 138; color of polyporus, 139; manner of making a
spore-print, 140-144; colors of
prints; high relief, 142; fixing the
prints, 143.
Mutilla ant, 197.

NASTURTIUM, 205.
Nature, check to rapid increase of,
195.
Nelumbo, water-lily, 45.
Nettle (*Celtis*), 154.
Nettle-leaf tent-builders, laying the
egg, 155; contents of the curled
leaf, 156; gray and spine-covered,
156; rapid change of home, 157;
another specimen of different
color, stingless, 158; size of full-
grown specimen; a surprise; preparing for the transformation,
159; an ever-interesting revelation; quaint golden ear-
drops, 160; an astonishing trick,
161.
New England farmers, 65.
Niagara Suspension-bridge, manner
of laying, 105; identical with that
of the spider, 106.
Noctiluca, marine phosphorescent
animalculæ, 21.
Noisy wigglers, 76.
Nymphæa, water-lily, 45.

OAK-apple, 43.
October rowen-fields, 116.
Odor of woods, 131.
Oil beetle. See Beetles.
Old rose, 73.
Orb-weavers, 120.
Orchard oriole, 172.
Osmoderma scabei, perfumed beetle,
134.
Ovid quoted, 93.

PANSIES (*Viola tricolor*):—Great variety of color, 46; trickery of florists; aniline bath, 47; a chemical experiment; astonishing color, 48; ammonia as an agent; coloring an entire plant emerald green, 50; results from the fumes of sulphur matches, 52.
Passion-flower, 189.
Passion-vine, 186.
Perfumed beetle (*Osmoderma scabei*), curious odor of, 133; suggesting Russia-leather; home on the maple-tree; sipping the sap; easily startled, 134.
Pink, 205.
Plant-louse of the apple-tree, 236.
Pliny, 64, 114, 116, 252.
Pollen bearers, 30.
Polyphemus. See Moths.
Polyporus, 144.
Preservation of food by wasps, 256.
Primrose ash, 73.
Professor of biology, 70.
"Professor Wiggler," what a florist's window suggested; the lilac-bush his home, 73; his characteristics, 74; how he came to be named; bringing him up by hand, 75; lively capers, 76; five changes of clothes; voracious feeding, 77; how he retains his head-shells, 78; digging out a home, 79; home completed; skilful concealment; what comes from the cocoon, 81; burrowing habits, 82.
Puff-balls, 136; its purple cloud, 136; rapid change of substance; its cloud mass of reproductive atoms, 137; same results from mushrooms and toadstools, 138.

Pungent odors, 132.

"QUAKER." See Grasshopper.

"RACER," 85.
Red Admiral. See Butterflies.
"Red-hot child of nature," 92, 96.
Redstart, 176.
Red-tailed hawk, 152, 153.
Riddles in flowers, 202; curious specimens; botanists and philosophers, 204; pollen-carrying, 207; galaxy of white or blue stars, 208; variety of construction, 209; solving the riddle, 211.
Riley, C. V., quoted, 254.
"Robin's pin-cushion," 43.
Roland for an Oliver, 59.
Roots, becoming stems and bearing leaves, 87.
Rose garden, 126.
Roses, blue, 45, 46; green, 187.
Rosy moth, 85.
Rowen-field, 116, 218.

SABBATH sanctuary bouquet, 26.
Sacred "scarabæus," emblem of immortality, 53.
Sage blossom, its welcome to the bee, 221.
Sand-hornet:—Prospecting for game, 249; the capture, 250; manner of transporting its prey, 251; its color and terrible sting, 252; not to be trifled with; its home in the sand-bank, 253; deposits its egg and leaves, 254; its mysterious poison, 256.
Scrophularia, figwort, 28.
Semicolon. See Butterflies.

Sheep-spit, 84.
Singular mimic fruit, 42.
Small speckled beetle, 86.
Smilax, 188.
Snake expert, 67.
Snake stories, 65.
Snake-spit, 84, 85.
Snapping beetle. See Beetles.
"Snowin' 'pider-webs," 113.
Sphinx caterpillar (*Chærocampa pampenatrix*) with his burden, 241, 242; the mischief-maker (*Microgaster*, 245.
Spice-bush, 131, 132.
Spiders, webs one hundred feet long; autumn best time for observation, 106; precocious baby spiders; building a bridge, 108; moored by guy threads, 110; ballooning, 112; at sea, 113.
Sponge-ball, commonly known as Bedegnar, 43.
Sprengel, 166, 202, 206.
"Spume-bearer" (*Aphrophora*), 89; allied to bugs; his aerated bath; graduation from his surroundings, 87; his color and size; his alertness, 88; time of egg-laying and hatching; power of leaping, 89; no secret process of making suds; sun's evaporation necessitates continuous additions, 90.
Squirrel, 153.
Statue of Liberty, 108.
Stems assuming the functions of roots, 187.
Summer meadows, 83.
Sweetbrier sponge, 40.
Sweet-pea, 188.

Tachina, a parasitic fly, 200.

Tendrils, what they are; a stem or modified root, 187; reaching for conquest, 188; not a special or primal organ, 189; method of contraction, 191; the reverse twist, its function, 192; singular botanical prank, 194.
Thelaphora cærulea, fox-fire, 22.
Tiger-beetle, wonderful speed and agility of, 2.
Toad-spit, 84.
Toadstools, 19, 138.
Trailing cobwebs, 113.
True locust, the, 232.
Tulip, blue, 45.
Tumble-bug, his former eminence, 53; used for ornaments and decorative purposes; his proud lineage, 54; male and female inseparable; the two familiar species; its season, 55; curious antics; bug talk, 56; a question of selection, 58; indefatigable workers; manner of working, 59; Mrs. Tumble-bug's industry, 60; singular manner of burying the ball, 61; the chrysalis state, 62; young Mr. Tumble-bug begins life, 63.
Twilight moth. See Moths.

UNION Square Fountain, 45.

VIREO, strange materials in the nest of, 147, 164, 171, 172.

WASPS, as cross-fertilizers, 30; manner of transferring pollen, 31, 91; "Digger," sand-hornets, 242, 252.
Weeds, artistically treated, 27; barn-yard weeds no longer commonplace, 28.

Welcome odor of the woods, 131.
Welcome of the flowers, 30, 223.
White, Gilbert, quoted, 114–117.
White, J., 161.
White Mountains, 97.
White-tailed black wasp, 94.
Wiggler moth (*Gramatophora trisignata*), time of appearance of, 81.
Wild-star cucumber, 189.
Witch-hazel divining-rod, 214.
Wolf-spiders, short-legged dodgers; crab-like manner of walking, 120.
Wood-fairies at work; their magic wands, 36; mischief-makers, 37; results of their pranks, 38.

Woolly-bear caterpillar. See Caterpillar.
Woolly flock, 230; expert in bugs, 231; what constitutes a bug, 232, 235; first appearance in June; on alders; destruction of apple-trees; sucking-beaks, 233; wingless but covered with woolly down, 236.
Worm-eating warbler, vireo, 164.

XANTHIC, flowers including yellow in their color, 45.

YELLOW geranium, 45.
Yellow larkspur, 45.
Yellow-jacket bee, 91.
Yellow-warbler, 171.

WILLIAM HAMILTON GIBSON'S WORKS.

ILLUSTRATED BY THE AUTHOR.

OUR EDIBLE TOADSTOOLS AND MUSHROOMS, and How to Distinguish Them. Thirty Colored Plates, and Fifty-seven other Illustrations. 8vo, Cloth, Uncut Edges and Gilt Top, $7 50. (*In a Box.*)

SHARP EYES. A Rambler's Calendar. *New Edition.* 8vo, Cloth, Ornamental, $2 50.

STROLLS BY STARLIGHT AND SUNSHINE. Royal 8vo, Cloth, Gilt Edges, $3 50.

HAPPY HUNTING-GROUNDS. A Tribute to the Woods and Fields. 4to, Cloth, Gilt Edges, $7 50. (*In a Box.*)

HIGHWAYS AND BYWAYS; or, Saunterings in New England. *New Edition.* 8vo, Cloth, Ornamental, $2 50.

PASTORAL DAYS; or, Memories of a New England Year. 4to, Cloth, Gilt Edges, $7 50. (*In a Box.*)

CAMP LIFE IN THE WOODS, and the Tricks of Trapping and Trap-making. 16mo, Cloth, $1 00.

PUBLISHED BY HARPER & BROTHERS, NEW YORK.

www.ingramcontent.com/pod-product-compliance
Lightning Source LLC
Chambersburg PA
CBHW032115230426
43672CB00009B/1748